D064322S

Running Barefoot

by

Susan Lang

Aakenbaaken & Kent

Running Barefoot

Copyright 2019, all rights reserved.

No part of this book may be used or reproduced in any manner whatsoever without written permission except in the case of brief quotations for use in articles and reviews.

Aakenbaakeneditor@gmail.com

ISBN: 978-1-938436-72-7

Praise for Susan Lang's previous works

Small Rocks Rising

"With an unconventional pioneer woman as its heroine, Lang's earnest, nostalgic debut novel explores the satisfactions of learning how to tame the wilderness. A homesteader in the 1920s, independent-minded Ruth Farley stakes her claim to a Southern California canyon, optimistically renaming her parcel of land Glory Springs. As she struggles to clear the land for building, a hard-to-move boulder becomes a metaphor for the struggles she faces in coping with querulous fellow homesteaders, dangerously aggressive men and her dawning romantic feelings for a local Indian. The desire for freedom pervades this tale of woman against environment freedom from oppressive social conventions and particularly from other people's ideas of femininity. Lang's writing can be fluid and evocative, especially when she's describing the landscape and the practical challenges of living in the wilderness." — *Publishers Weekly*

"Susan Lang has created a vision of the world steeped in wildness and in compassion for nature, and for the positive cultures that sustain us. Her vision is one of hope, hope that is embodied in her courageous heroine, Ruth Farley, a wonderful woman who is simply in love with life. Don't just read this novel, read the entire trilogy: Its blessings are multiple, entertaining, and uplifting." — John Nichols, author of *The Milagro Beanfield War*

Juniper Blue

"To Lang's credit, Ruth stays in character with her practical, physical, reactionary, stubborn, straight-speaking, passionate, changeable, not-always-likeable persona; and she avoids floating off into spiritual, supernatural or man-dependent realms. Lang doesn't freight the blue horse with symbolic or spiritual meaning (although readers could find it themselves); she doesn't assign unrealistic spiritual power to the Yuiatei people; and she doesn't fall back on romance-genre convention.... But real love in *Juniper Blue* occurs between Ruth and her land, and Lang depicts it in polished, authentic, evocative prose." — Christine Wald-Hopkins, *Tucson Weekly*

"What a double gift: the return of Southwestern novelist Susan Lang and the return of her heroine, Ruth Farley. Both Susan and Ruth epitomize the tender fierceness required to live in wilderness—wilderness of the heart, wilderness of spirit and those intersections of desert light, rock and longing that can destroy a woman, or restore her to her life. *Juniper Blue* came to me at a time when I had to face the impact of a hiking fall, metaphorically and physically. Ruth Farley reminded me that where there is breath, there is hope; where there is courage, there is deep love. Where there is desert beneath my feet, there are blessings beyond measure." — Mary Sojourner

The Sawtooth Complex

"*The Sawtooth Complex* is a fascinating novel that deals vigorously with the dilemmas of human life of the planet. Our willy-nilly destruction of the exquisite natural world is set against the efforts of some people to protect and care for the biology that sustains us. Most characters are torn by contradictions, both personal and political. A few are avid developers; others week a balance between humanity and nature. Several touching love stories develop and falter among them. The true hero, Maddie Farley, is an inspiring and reluctant monkey-wrencher who lives most closely to the earth. The natural world she inhabits is invoked with poignant accuracy and love. Ultimately, nature itself blows up everyone's world in a startling forest fire that overpowers the land and the people, laying waste to most everything. The writing about this thrilling climactic event is terrifying, spellbinding, very intense and powerful. And then a miracle occurs. In the wreckage left behind, the author, who is not sentimental idealist or doomsday prophet, finds reason to hope. The story is engrossing, entertaining, and really makes us think. It's a find addition to our best environmental and human–humane–literature." John Nichols, author of *The Milagro Beanfield War*

In God's Trailer Park

"The compassionate courage vibrates on every page, making the novel sing out with hopefulness during tragic and heartbreaking times. We need Susan Lang's vision of caring for the future."
—John Nichols, author of *The Milagro Beanfield War*

"It's a story with all the old virtues—strong characters involved in vivid incidents, surviving wounds and partial healings . . . I came out of the reading sorry to be finished . . ." —William Kittredge

"Lang's characters ring with authenticity, humor and heart. In God's Trailer Park is utterly endearing." — Michaela Carter, Author of *Further Out Than You Thought*

Dedication

For Carol Houck Smith

Chapter One
Naked into the Wild
1972

"After all the money I spent so you can go to that goddamn university, and now you're trying to get expelled over a stupid war protest?" Daryl lets the newspaper drift to the floor. It's the latest issue of *The Root*, an underground student newspaper I contribute to. He'd snatched it from my pile of papers when he saw the front page photo of our entire staff lined up, black-armband-side-out, defying the administration's threat to expel students who dared protest the Vietnam slaughterhouse.

I feel my temperature rise. "*You* spent? You don't contribute a penny. I've brought in over six thousand this year with loans and scholarships–that's as much as you make. And double what I'd be bringing in as a waitress. Even my tuition is scholarshipped. Besides, you'd be happy if I got expelled–which I won't."

"Yeah, yeah, yeah. All that still doesn't pay for the gas," he said, somehow managing to stomp his boot down on the photo of faces. "Or for the motor I had to put in that damn VW bug."

"You had to put in? Sonny's Garage put that motor in. Dad told us it needed a new motor when he gave it to me for my birthday." I can't stop my voice from rising, "so I *could* go to school." I take in a deep breath, try to calm myself. But he just won't shut up.

"So what?" he says now. "It still cost me four hundred bucks to put the son-of-a bitch in."

"Three fifty–and I paid for it with my scholarship money."

"It doesn't matter what you say, Sue. You know the truth as well as I do – everything you have, you owe to me." He says this without the least sign of irony. Not that Daryl is capable of irony.

"Oh," I say, blood rushing to my head. If I weren't so angry, I might be amused. This guy wouldn't even be employed if it weren't for my father's painting business. "Is that so?"

I take a deep breath, look out the window at the wild land surrounding our house, and remember the years of running free as a child in the wash of the canyon homestead, clad only in cotton panties. Each brush of sole a kiss from the warm sand, silky from eons of floods. The joy of it washes over me. "All right then," I say.

I whip my midriff top up over my head and fling it onto the sofa, unbutton my jeans, peeling them down along with my panties, then step out of my *huaraches*. For good measure, I even roll off the black armband and toss it into the air.

"Well, here you are, then. All yours." I swing my hair back over my shoulders and march toward the back door, aware of my jiggling breasts, and of my fine ass waving him an unfond farewell.

"Don't be stupid." He follows me as far as the door.

"Just let her go, Dad," I hear Renee say, an eye-roll audible in her teenage twit voice. But better a twit than pregnant like I was at fifteen. Pregnant with her. Timmy's and Kim's eyes don't even leave the TV. Our other two, Linda and Jimmy, are off playing in the back bedroom.

"You stay home, Simi," I tell our part-greyhound mutt as I head off toward the knoll behind the abandoned house where we'd been squatting for the past year. It's an older house above the town golf course, and the nicest house we've ever lived in, one we'd actually rented legitimately and cheaply the last time we lived here, a couple of years before. I love the living room's quartz rock wall with the fireplace, the high ceiling with its thick cross-beams, and the whole wall of windows on each side of the living room. The kids like it because the place has TV reception–unlike most of the houses we'd lived in. We do have to have water hauled in to the tank on the knoll, but I'd been raised to conserve water on mother's homestead. Otherwise our spring would go dry and we'd have to wait hours for it to replenish.

The house is private, too, on the periphery of Yucca Valley, a small Mojave Desert town of three thousand located over a hundred miles from the LA area. The land around us is still the wild and undeveloped desert landscape I feel most at home in. Of course, being wild means the place is infested with tarantulas, mice and pack rats who had been inhabiting the desert mountains and empty house long before we arrived. A year or so ago, we'd simply moved back into the house, thinking the out-of-town owner would find out and contact us. We still haven't heard from him. Rumor had it that he was traveling somewhere in Europe. Good thing, too. The money we'd saved on rent did help pay for my gas to drive the ninety miles to the university in Riverside two days a week.

Or maybe the owner is just waiting for the tarantulas to get us.

I sprint up the knoll next to the house, then up the ridge toward the higher peak, enjoying the feel of my bare feet touching down and lifting off from the granite sand, the light wind cooling the sweat on my skin. I run as I did at age four, five, six, seven on the wild canyon homestead. As I did at nine, ten, eleven, twelve, running clothed now but feet still free from shoes.

Pure joy lifts me above small sage and buckwheat as I maneuver my way to the larger mountain and zigzag easily up the ridge toward the spring, avoiding the hard spears of Spanish Dagger and stinging spines of Cholla. Lizards scamper away in front of me. My callused soles prove their worth on the rough soil of the mountain as I fly forward, then as now, running forth to explore the unfolding day and put distance between myself and the conflict behind me.

I'd learned young to run from someone whose unhappiness served as a swamp to bog me down. It was harder with Daryl; I'd been only fifteen when we married, and it had taken many years for me to understand that I could not heal his wounds, and that his way of healing was to grab every chance to wound me. Now, after 15 years I was seeking my own joy and no longer concerned about fostering his. I had tourniqueted myself off to stop the bleeding and no longer let his chronic sneak attacks affect me.

Today, each step I place against the warm granite sand gives me a surge of power. I imagine myself absorbing the energy I need to survive from the earth under my soles. Running barefoot makes me feel free and fully alive, the sun, too, energizing my tanned body. I could live on acorns, piñon nuts, and pigweed if I needed to, dig out springs from damp and grassy places I've known since childhood, I think to myself, ignoring the deer flies that follow to bite my bare butt and gnats that attack my eyes, and the fact that the quality of decomposed granite sand is much harsher to run on than the fine satin sand in the washes of my childhood.

Actually, living off the land might have been doable for me in those days, but I'd already done enough of that sort of thing, despite my feelings at the moment. I'd spent most of my childhood years in that wild and isolated canyon. That was one reason I'd gone back to school at age twenty-eight, after twelve years of being a high school dropout who worked as a waitress between – and sometimes during – pregnancies that had resulted in five children before I turned twenty-three. By the time of my naked run that day, I'd already spent two years at the university after transferring from a year at a community college.

I slow when I reach the top of the peak and jog along the ridge on the other side, heading in the direction of my mother's homestead a few miles away. It's not my plan, however, to travel all the way over those mountains to that empty cabin, even if my feet have remained nearly tough enough to walk on cactus all the way. I'd grown up barefoot on that homestead. Even now I went barefoot every chance I got, around town and to grocery stores, even attended classes barefoot when I felt like it. You could still do that back in 1972, at least at California colleges. Now at age thirty, my disdain for shoes had grown philosophic underpinnings–for me shoes symbolized all the things we humans used to buffer ourselves from experiencing the world in its true wildness.

I had no plan that day for my naked excursion into the mountains. No conscious plan, anyway. Plans were a luxury in those days–something that worked for others who had more stable lives, but never worked out in mine. You might say I negotiated my way though life using creative instincts and staying sensitive to possibilities that appeared in what experience had taught me was an ever-changing and unpredictable present over which I had little control. That's the way my life had been from the start.

Maybe my attending college the past three years had been a way to finally control something in my life. When I dropped out of high school at the end of my freshman year of high school, I told people I would go to college some day, though no one believed me. Sometimes I even doubted it myself. But twelve years later, when my youngest started kindergarten, it seemed like the time had come to do it. What better place for me to be with the world in flux and about to change? The world of injustice and meaningless wars *needed* to change. And I wanted to help change it. My black armband was a symbol of that–a small sacrifice, it seemed, compared to what others were making. Not only all the young men sacrificed by the draft, but the four students dead and nine wounded at Kent State last month by US troops. Despite what Daryl said, I didn't really believe the university would expel hundreds of students for wearing black arm bands, especially after Kent State. Besides, my second year at the university was already over, and I was a newly sworn-in Phi Beta Kappa.

The truth was I still had a lot to learn about that bigger world outside of Yucca Valley that I wanted to see changed, despite all books I'd read about it. After all, our family only occasionally had TV, and radio reception in our desert town was not much to speak of. The kind of life I'd lived myself had, for the most part, taught me how to thrive in dire circumstances, like a desert plant. Yet it didn't take much knowledge to see the injustice and inequality in that world that needed to change. Of course, my life needed changing as well, something harder to do without planning–but not impossible.

When I think about it, I'm amazed that I ever made it through college. Not just because I had to drag an unwilling Daryl and our hard-scrabble life along with me and make sure I didn't neglect our five children in the process. But also because I went through the whole thing without an academic plan of any kind. Getting a degree had never been the goal of my return to school. My real reason to go to college was to learn more–but especially to finally discuss the ideas I'd been encountering in books for those twelve years of reading at home. I'd always found learning delicious–whether from books or from the wild I grew up in. But life just sort of funneled me in the direction of degreehood.

Take my experience with Phi Beta Kappa. All during the previous year at the university, my junior year, I had become more and more annoyed at all the letters I was receiving that invited me to join this or that Greek honor society, organizations I disdained as elitist. I reveled in an intellectual arrogance most likely born out of the powerlessness over my life. In such arrogance, I felt I was far above such bourgeois honor organizations. I tossed each and every invitation into the trash as soon as I realized what it was. I didn't understand how these organizations kept getting my name, though, since I wasted no time socializing during the two class-packed days per week I spent at the university. Any time I did have between classes I used for discussing and exploring ideas gleaned from books and interpretations of the literary works from classes–usually with my friend Gary–or anyone else I could interest in talking theory.

One "invitation" I received, however, did more than invite–

the letter claimed to have actually *elected* me into itself. I was outraged, so outraged that I phoned my older sister, Bobette, in LA – Bobette had married and escaped Mother's clutches when I was three.

"How dare they elect me without my permission," I repeated after I had ranted for some time about all the honor societies hounding me. "How do I get them to stop?"

"What did you say the name was? Of the one that elected you, I mean?" Bobette asked.

"Oh, I don't know. I think it was Phi Beta something or other. Kappa, I think." I asked my sister if an organization could really do that, elect me into it without my permission, then "invite" me to pay some kind of twenty dollar key fee.

I remember the long silence before she said, "Do you still have that letter?"

"Probably. I haven't emptied the trash yet." I hardly ever emptied bedroom trash can until crumpled pages of paper drafts spilled out onto the floor.

"Go see if you do."

So I put down the phone and dug out the wadded up letter from the trash to verify the name. Bobette then took it upon herself to enlighten me about a few possible benefits. Accepting the so-called election might actually bring jobs when I got my degree, and so forth. Jobs? Degree? That got my attention. In my obsession with wanting to learn more and explore ideas, I hadn't thought much about education's practical applications, but I did know I was awfully tired of being a waitress.

"Okay, okay," I said. "But I can't just throw away twenty dollars like that. I don't have it. If I did I'd buy shoes for the kids."

By the time the twenty dollars Bobette sent me arrived in the mail, I had, thanks to the help of my dear school buddy, Gary, added up all my credits and learned that I only had another year left before I could get a B.A. All I needed now, he said, were a few easy courses I had skipped to take juicier ones, dense with ideas. Maybe with a degree I really could get one of those "good" jobs my sister had talked about, one I enjoyed doing. Perhaps even rent a nice house for us to live in rather than squat in one. Buy all of us new shoes and even clothes occasionally, instead of swapping out their old worn outfits for newer used ones at the coop clothes exchange.

It's hard now for me to understand that the idea of having the power to transform my actual living conditions – rather than simply spending my time exploring intellectual theories on the meaning of existence – was so alien to me. One reason for this blindness might have been my disinterest in material circumstances, something I must have gleaned from living in the wild. It wasn't that the material world didn't interest me but that what I found valuable in it resided in the natural world around me, not in furniture and fancy clothes. Yet over the years I had come to understand how important it was to at least have at least the basics for my children.

Perhaps that's why I didn't stay naked on the mountain that day to begin a new life as a wild woman. And not just because later a helicopter from the local Marine base started circling while I sat naked on a rough rock, trying to pry a cholla burr from my not-quite-tough-enough foot. I remember wishing I still had my armband – and, yes, even the rest of my clothes. I remember returning the recruits' enthusiastic waves with a dual-digit wave of my own – hoping they would understand I only meant it metaphorically. And I didn't go back home either just because a rattlesnake almost ended my plans, either. I think what made me go back was the fact that I only had a year left at the university and the hope that I could make a better life for myself and my children. So, eventually I circled back and waited for Daryl to make his late afternoon trip to the liquor store. Then I went home to cook some dinner for my hungry children and famished self.

Chapter Two
Drop Out Life
1965

It is seven years earlier and I'm squatting again, only this time literally, in the middle of the street in front of the house we live in at the other edge of the same small desert town. I'm twenty-three and little Jimmy, my fifth child, is only a few months old. I'd been curled up in the bedroom, reading Jean Paul Sartre's *Being and Nothingness*, and was just about ready to slip into a nothingness of my own since I'd only had about three hours sleep after my shift at the café before the kids woke up that morning. But a god-awful screech of tires, a thump, then a cacophony of yelps outside woke me up fast. Then more tire screeching. I sprang up and ran outside in an explosion of adrenalin, envisioning the two toddlers – my toddlers – that I'd heard laughing in the yard only a moment before, now mangled in the road.

Any thought I might have had of creating meaning in my life or consciously choosing my *being* were left lying there on the bed with Sartre's book. The reality I knew didn't leave much room for conscious choices anyway, as I saw it. At least it had always seemed that way. Life was just one crisis after another to solve or to just get through.

Thank god it wasn't Linda and Kim, but a German Sheppard thrashing wildly in the street. The poor thing had been hanging around the last few days, begging for scraps. A cream-colored station wagon was just disappearing around the corner. I squatted down to assess the dog's injury just as my next door neighbor Sharon came running over to see what had happened. Sharon started to cry the minute she saw the way the dog's head had been split open and a dash of its brain mashed onto the pavement. Its yelps were quieting some now, its legs only jerking in occasional spasms. She knelt beside the dog and stroked its side. The kids, mine – she didn't have any – were standing by our fence, all of them crying, too.

I sprang up and ran to get the .22 from under the front seat of the Ford. I'd hidden the rifle there a couple days earlier, after Daryl told me how he'd almost used it to shoot Sharon while I was at work. According to Daryl, he and Sharon had had a wildly passionate kissing session that stopped short of sex one night when she asked him over to help her reach something. He also said that while I was at work she kept walking back and forth in front of our house, hoping he'd come out and at least talk to her again. The thing was, I had no idea whether or not this is the truth, or just another one of the many stories he tells so I will spend hours listening to him complain and blame. Most of the stories he tells seem to be in order to hide his activities from me. Yet I knew he really might be going through another psychotic episode, like the one he had after his father died three years ago, and the possibility of him shooting Sharon seemed far too serious to take a chance with. The very idea of it made my neck hairs prickle. That's why I'd confiscated the rifle. Meanwhile, Sharon was clueless that Daryl might be cracking up and plotting her demise.

When I returned to the street, the dog was still whimpering and twitching. "Stay back," I told Sharon. Before she could get fully to her feet, I cocked and aimed the gun at the suffering dog's forehead, and was just about to pull the trigger when I heard another horrid screech of tires down the street. I looked over in time to see my brother's jeep come careening around the corner – taking with him half the picket fence from around the vacant corner house.

The dog let out a loud yelp of pain. I turned back, aimed the .22 between the poor things eyes and pulled the trigger just as my fifteen year old brother pulled up. He leapt from his jeep, leaving the driver's door wide open and the vehicle jerking to a stop on its own.

"Stop! Don't do it, Susie. Don't do it," he yelled as he ran toward me. He yanked the gun from my hands.

"But his brain was mashed and the poor thing was in pain, Danny. I had to."

My brother looked from me to the dog and then to Sharon, who'd barely had time to get out of the way. Confusion spread over his face. Suddenly I understood his panic and started to laugh. I could see from his face that he now realized his mistake. He began to laugh as well.

"Now why didn't I think of that?" I said, laughing even harder, so hard I finally had to sit down beside the dead dog to keep from wetting my pants.

The kids had stopped crying and were looking at the two of us like they couldn't quite believe what they were seeing. So was Sharon – which made me laugh even harder. I knew they had to think we were the ultimate in cruelty. But what were we going to do? Tell them that Danny saw me and thought I was about to shoot Sharon because of the near affair and had come rushing over to save me from doing it? Shit, Sharon should be able to figure that out on her own.

I could see why Danny might think that, too. I had confided in him about Daryl and Sharon's encounter only yesterday after I'd had to rescue him from a real affair of his own. He had confessed the affair when I picked him up at the phone booth. The affair had been with his Sunday school teacher, who also happened to be the wife of the veterinarian, who was also a John Birch survivalist, that my brother he worked for after high school. A few weeks before, the day after Danny's fifteenth birthday, the guy had actually hired him to hide half of his gun collection in a cave on the mountain in a place that only my brother knew about. That way the guns would be available after the communists took over.

The vet still had the other half of his gun collection in the house and had been using them to snipe at my brother here and there around town, after he found out about the affair. Which is why I'd picked Danny up at the phone booth outside of the drugstore and hid him for the afternoon. The story my kid brother told me that day had by far outclassed any stories *I* had on hand, and so I'd offered up the only one I did have, which was about Daryl and Sharon.

As we stood there laughing beside the poor mangled dog, some part of me was aware that it would never have occurred to me to shoot Sharon that day. And on top of it all, the reason I'd been hiding the gun in a place I'd have it with me at work was so *Daryl* wouldn't shoot her. All that irony made the situation seem even more absurd. Maybe more like Kafka than Sartre, I thought to myself (who else in my life would have understood?). Then I wondered what an intellectual like Jean Paul would have said and done if he were here in my position, and the sheer impossibility of such a thing made me howl even louder. The gap between the life I lived and the sophisticated lives depicted in books I read seemed insurmountable.

I looked over at Sharon, who now had a 'no-wonder-Daryl-wants-*me*' look on her face, with shades of 'who are these people, anyway?'

If she or anyone else *had* asked that question, I would have had no idea what to say. I, myself, would never have thought to ask myself such a question. I tended to think of myself more in terms of *what* I was: a creature living on this planet spinning through time and space who read everything she could get her hands on in order to understand what she and everyone else were doing here in the first place. What was the meaning of our being here? Was there a meaning? And what did I mean by meaning? I don't think I spent much time applying that to what was going on in my own everyday life.

While I could 'talk the talk' eloquently about the *concept* of creating one's self out of conscious actions, I had little thought of implementing such a questionable concept in my own life and zero faith in its viability in the life I knew. I was more intent on discovering new ideas in books. I hadn't read the psychologists yet – though I was just about to discover them as I tried to understand what was happening with Daryl. Even as I read Sartre, I had no idea who I was in the sense the question is usually meant – and never would have thought to ask the question. I was twenty-three; I had birthed five children in seven years, using various inefficient forms of pre-pill contraceptive devices and practices, and now I was trying to fine the meaning of life here on this planet as it traveled through the universe.

Meaning, as it actually occurred in my life – aside from finding amazing ideas in books and caring for my children – was not an abstraction. It came in the form of the joy I felt watching the sky at night, a window into infinite wonder; in seeing, smelling, touching the rainbow of fragile flowers that managed to make their appearance in the dry desert spring; in observing the behavior of fellow creatures – insects and lizards and snakes and rabbits and plants and everything else; in seeing the wonder in everything everywhere in the wild desertscape.

I suppose thumbing my nose at the hardscrabble realities of my life with Daryl was made possible by my intellectual pursuits, by retaining the looks I'd had before having any children, back when I was fourteen and modeled bathing suits for local boutiques. (Keeping one's looks wasn't that hard to do at twenty-three.) I was just under five feet, my hair was still long, and I had made it blonder and blonder as it darkened. In short, I made sure I *appeared* as if none of what had happened the last few years with Daryl and the children had affected me at all.

At the same time, I remember being keenly aware (usually when I looked at myself in a mirror) that my physical self was transitory and a trap if I based my identity on it – and that a real and authentic self needed to have more substance. Maybe that was because since around the time my second child was born when I was seventeen, I had been letting my mind and imagination run barefoot through book after book. Each was a new adventure, a new place to explore. I took every book seriously, sometimes coming back from my journeys changed forever.

My reading quest had begun at age seventeen with the Bible. I don't remember why. Perhaps I sensed that I'd somehow lost my way – or began to wonder for the first time if there might be a path out there somewhere that didn't lead to being pregnant with a third child while trapped in a marriage with an unreliable and untrustworthy partner. Daryl had already had at least one affair I knew of (while I was pregnant with my first baby), and I had kept finding out about lie after lie he told concerning just about everything. I must have known I needed to do something because I had tried to register for a high school night class around that time, but with my night job as a waitress and a baby and toddler to care for during the day, it was much easier just to read during their naps.

It's easy to see why the concept of taking control of my life – let alone shaping my being – was foreign to me at this point. Like most children of my era, which was not the child-centered era we have now, where life took me had been determined by the needs and whims of my parents, more specifically in my case, by the whims of my mother to get back to her canyon and, for various reasons I never fully understood, to leave it again. Even the decision for me to marry Daryl had been my parents.' When my father confronted Daryl with a gun the night we returned from our grape-picking adventure, Daryl told my parents that I was pregnant so we needed to get married. And even when tests revealed that I wasn't, they decided that because I was already 'ruined' from having sex. I should marry him anyway and was lucky he still wanted me. No one even asked me.

I was pretty much invisible, confused and lost in the shuffle. I had realized during the grape-picking adventure that it wasn't the romantic life I'd envisioned after reading *Grapes of Wrath*, and that Daryl was no *Rebel-Without-A Cause*-like James Dean, and had returned home thinking I might somehow slip back into my normal life, painful though it would be. Maybe I believed my parents would save me from myself. Fat chance of that after being "ruined."

Two years and two babies later, at seventeen, I began my reading quest. By that time, I had lost all sense of myself as the barefoot runner, eager explore new places and meet whatever the day or life had in store for me, that sense of myself – perhaps born of bravado – I'd always had as someone who would dispatch any rattler that got in her way. Or for that matter put any suffering animal out of its misery. I was lost and confused living in a city, lost in my role of a teen mother of two, who was vulnerable to the erratic whims of a husband I could never trust. So I picked up the book I'd loved for all its New Testament stories and parables in Sunday School and started reading it from the beginning, perhaps hoping it would show me the way back to my earlier self.

But when I got to the Old Testament that Bible had another effect on me, entirely. Just who was this powerfully cruel and punishing Judaic God who was the Book's main character, I began to wonder? I was outraged that this cruel and angry guy was in charge of everything. I disliked him intensely. He was nothing like the Jesus I'd loved and respected – though he sure could stand to learn a few lessons from his son! Around the same time I also happened upon a book in the library about the historical context of the Bible and read about the way the Judaic god concept grew out of the volcano gods and such. That revelation along with the shock of encountering God as depicted in the Old Testament left me a raging atheist. I wanted no part of an afterlife ruled by such a terrible being. It would be a long time before my rage would be tempered by the realization that what I was seeing was really the historical human concept of the immense powers we did not understand and had no control over.

I progressed to my mother's set of The Great Books of the Western World, the density of Aristotle, Plato and Herodotus was wonderfully relieved with works by Shakespeare, Tolstoy,

Dostoevsky, Melville, Homer and others. Then on to more and more places, other books, that I searched out. I was interested only in important books, including the classics of world fiction, that might have answers about life – even if I could hardly understand what some of them were saying without knowing more about the eras they were written in. This led me to stop and do as much reading to find out about the historical context as I could without being near a major library. I would also take pauses to read the rest of some authors' works I loved that I could find or order in libraries, authors such as Tolstoy, Dostoevsky and others. Also, reading Hegel and Kant sent me to find other philosophers, sometimes more current philosophers, which I had been doing when I encountered Sartre.

My quest for meaning and knowledge at the time was not at all internal. And such a thing was not a part of the rural culture I was part of. Being, not thinking, had always been my way of staying happy in my own life or at least okay. So dragging my bed out into the yard on summer nights to track the moon and stars and think about the meaning and wonders of life in the abstract was plenty good enough for me.

If I had given who I was a thought, I, as a character in my life, might have noticed not only the chasm between my intellectual life and my everyday life, but also the split between the two main areas that nurtured and sustained me – my absolute need to draw sustenance from both my intellectual life, where I felt myself a part of some great conversation, and from the wild, untamed physical world I was part of. Both had plenty to teach me, more than I could ever learn.

Without these two crucial passions, how could I possibly have gotten through the sleep-deprived nights working until the wee hours as a waitress between pregnancies, then having to get up with kids at 5 or 6:00 am? How else could I have survived intact the heartache and ego blows I experienced during those pregnancies when sometimes Daryl didn't come home for days, or the time I opened the trunk of our '55 Ford to find blankets and beer bottles and several strange pairs of panties and bras? Or the times Daryl was fired because he ripped off prescription drugs or other things from the peoples' houses he painted? Those worlds of wild forces and intriguing ideas and lives helped buffer the ego blows, the fears and sadness that came from Daryl's lies and cheating, and grounded me to deal with Daryl's many psychotic episodes, where he became delusional, sometimes hallucinating his dead evil father, the hallucinations I suspected had been going on again while he was threatening to shoot our next door neighbor, Sharon.

My love of books and ideas and the wild around me helped keep me from delving into sordid events I could do little about. I supposed it also kept me from wondering why I stayed stuck in this situation for so damned long, kids or no kids. I never had much time for pondering such things as my own motivations, anyway, even if I'd wanted to, caught as I was without resources on the endless treadmill solving crisis after crisis to survive. Any time I did have to think, I spent speculating about the ideas I encountered in books, in interacting with my children, and in letting the wonder of the wild desert world raise my spirits. That was a way I could leap over some of the cactus patches and rattlers that kept appearing in my path, in other words, the actual life I lived in.

I was quick to find moments of joy in small things. I remember a one such time about a week after Linda, my fourth, was born. I'd had to go back out and get a job as a waitress again when she was four days old since Daryl had post-partum depression and decided to quit his job. We still had to eat. I was just glad he felt well enough get up and watch the kids once I put them to bed and left for work.

Anyway, after a busy Friday dinner rush at Sugar's Café, without a moment to breathe, my breasts were leaking milk through the paper towels I'd stuffed into my bra, and I was so tired and sore that I began to wonder if my womb might just fall out between my legs and go splat on the tile floor. Yet I walked out the door of the restaurant after closing feeling elated and filled with the joy of being alive. Why? Because when I emptied the soup tureen for the night, I noticed that, although all the other vegetables stayed at the bottom of the tureen, the bits of celery floated right up to the top. No way could anyone keep that celery down. I saw an ontological miracle in that simple fact that lasted me for months. In fact, it still visits me at times. That was the kind of thing that sustained and lifted my thoughts skyward. Self-reflection might have sent my spirits to the bottom of the tureen.

Besides, as I said, self-reflection had never played a role in the cultural dynamic of the family I grew up in. I'd been trained to look outward to understand things, and it behooved me do to so. That's where the danger lurked. At least that's what I believed at the time.

And there actually were plenty of external dangers lurking in that wild canyon where I spent most of my childhood, and it was crucial to stay alert for it. The place was certainly not a park. I truly don't know how many times I found myself leaping over a rattler that I suddenly spied in my path. Cougars sometimes screamed from the darkness at night, and although running across bears, bobcats, coyotes, and even those cougars as I explored the mountains was rare, it did happen occasionally. Every day was a brand new adventure. I'd learned to keep my eyes and ears and even nostrils open. A core part of me was always on alert, observing and loving the world around me, loving even its dangers. I suppose finding clumps of rabbit fur or bird feathers and wings in the cold spring water at daybreak helped to bring an indelible awareness of the life-and-death struggle in that place.

Chapter Three
1941
Hollywood

I wasn't actually born in the wilderness that I grew up in, but in a hospital like most other mid-twentieth century American babies. When my parents married, my father managed to drag Mother away from the canyon and the life she loved to live on the outskirts of Hollywood. Love does have its costs, and the two of them must have loved each other, at least at the beginning. And most likely Mother really had no choice but to leave the homestead once she married, since the deed was in her first husband's name. Although her first husband may actually have been her second husband if one were to count a marriage annulled in El Paso that she never told anyone about. (I only found out about it by discovering a yellowed newspaper clipping stuck away in one of mother's old books on a cabin shelf when I was a child and have always wished that, instead of guiltily sticking it back and forgetting even which book it was in, I had kept track of it, perhaps secreted it away to probe in the future.)

The only way Mother had managed to qualify for that hundred and sixty-acre parcel to homestead in the first place was as a WWI veteran. Of course, *she* wasn't WWI vet, having been only seven when the war started. In order to file the claim, she had entered into a totally platonic (according to her) marriage with an older man named Kit, who *was* a WWI vet. The claim had been registered in his name. The vet never actually lived in the canyon, but he had furnished the materials and helped her build the homestead cabin needed to "prove up" on her claim. He remained living in the L.A. area, where he worked as a mechanic, coming out occasionally on weekends to bring her groceries and other essentials. This was a great arrangement for her, leaving her free to live her life as she saw fit the rest of the time. And live life she did, staying as wild and free as the place itself. The only obstacle to her freedom was a five-year old daughter (of forever mysterious patrilineage – but perhaps from the annulled marriage?) she had brought with her when she hitchhiked from El Paso a few years before, when the child was a toddler. This child was my older sister, Bobette, born when Mother was seventeen, more than fourteen years before I came on the scene.

As far as Bobette was concerned, Kit was her father, the only one she had ever known. He represented stability and kindness in her life, the way my father later did for me. If Bobette were telling this story, I'm sure she would have other, equally unflattering, things to say about Mother's behavior during those homestead days. But this is not her story but mine, some of it gleaned, it is true, from Bobette.

Actually, having a child with her didn't cramp Mother's style all that much. I learned from Bobette very different stories than the ones Mother recounted to me. From Bobette, I heard how at times Mother would leave her alone for days at a time in that remote canyon, when my sister was only five or six. According to Bobette, this would happen whenever some handsome cowboy would ride by and invite Mother to go with him to a "dance" in Big Bear or in god-knew-where. There were plenty of handsome cowboys around, which earned Mother quite a reputation with townsfolk. Her living in a cabin twelve miles (by a rough-hewn rut road) from the tiny town of Yucca Valley – then called Lone Star, surrounding population under 50 – didn't manage to stop the gossip.

Being left alone in the wild canyon miles from anyone as a young child was hard for my sister to deal with. She told me how during those times when she was left alone for the night, she would run back and forth from the cabin to the far bend in the late afternoon until she was so tired she could hardly walk. That way she might be able to fall asleep and maybe not lie awake terrified by whatever lurked in that mysterious darkness.

I doubt my young mother fully realized the impact her behavior was having on my sister; after a couple beers and massive hormonal assaults, the lines must have blurred. For five-year-old Bobette, appreciating Mother's gutsy behavior living in the wilderness and understanding that she was only acting out of her own neglected childhood wasn't possible. And the worst event was yet to come.

That worst event was the day Salty the sailor showed up in my Mother's life. Salty had been discharged – dishonorably – from the Navy he had joined at age sixteen and was now building roads with the WPA (The Works Progress Administration, part of Roosevelt's New Deal) while his parents were homesteading one of the new forty acre desert parcels given out to the poor during that time. Salty's parents' parcel just happened to lie at the mouth of Mother's canyon. Salty was a city boy from the slums of Chicago and must have seemed fairly exotic to my mother when they hooked up. Having been born and raised in El Paso, Mother was Southwest desert from head to toe. But the handsome sailor wanted more than just a few fun times with the wild woman of Pipes Canyon. My sister claims it was food that he wanted, food that her father provided. She told me of all the times Salty came up canyon to chow down on those groceries – sometimes even hiding in the trunk of Mother's car when they passed the Swedes' place on her way home. The Swedes, as locals called the collection of miners from Sweden who squatted in a rock house they built four miles down canyon from the homestead, were the closest and only neighbors.

In love and maybe a bit tired of her freedom, Mother divorced Kit, the man who had been a father to Bobette, and married the man who was to become my father. And they moved to the outskirts of Hollywood. California being a communal property state, in the divorce agreement, Mother was given joint title to the homestead, and Kit, who continued living in Hollywood, retained his half. Things must have been awkward at first, but they seemed have settled down some before I was born, three years later. By the time I was three, Kit came to live with us after he had a heart attack, and he moved with us back to the canyon when I was four, right after my younger sister Carolyn was born. We knew him as Uncle Kit. The stormy scowl on my father's face when Uncle Kit was around made it clear how he felt about the situation. The tension there was clear before I ever had an inkling about the history that explained it.

Even though my first four years on the planet were based in Hollywood, from the start my life departed from that of the average mid-twentieth-century city child. This was because our lives weren't spent solely in Hollywood. In fact, Mother insisted on spending every spring through fall living in a tent back at the homestead. Her original cabin had been burned by intruders, so we stayed those summers in an army tent under some shady piñons, a spot she called Indian Campground. Mother maintained that the place was actually an old Indian campground, but who knows? While the Indians who for hundreds of years *had* spent late summers in the canyon hunting deer and harvesting piñon nuts and camping around the spring on the mountain we now called ours, it was the cowboys coming through on cattle drives who had built up the old campfires and hung tin cans from the piñon branches to catch the pitch. They had named the place Can Tree Springs, which my mother promptly changed to Bahai d'Ola then to Echo Bend when she became afraid someone would think she was a Jew.

I was eight months old the first summer we spent on the homestead. Mother had worked hard to persuade my father to let her spend the summer there, even with "the baby," and, although he didn't like the arrangement one bit, he agreed to drive the hundred and twenty-some miles to bring us supplies every weekend. We stayed in the isolated canyon without a car or real dwelling, Mother cooking on a campfire and hauling water from the spring across the wash. She was back in her element.

I can't say I remember much about that very first summer when I was only a baby. Years later, though, I heard more about the first night my parents arrived with me, and the three of us slept out in the open, under the stars. How we hadn't gotten there until twilight and found it too late to set up the large army tent they'd brought. How the two of them simply raked away all the spiny piñon pine needles and spread a blanket for us to sleep on, Dad, Mother, and me off to the side a few feet away.

The next morning, the story went, they awoke to find mountain lion tracks in the freshly raked earth, tracks that took the lion right across the blanket where baby me slept, then away on the other side.

By the time I heard this story, I'd already spent years having a recurring dream where I went searching for something that I was mysteriously connected to – something that always turned out to be a huge mountain lion that I would finally discover above me, its glowing green eyes staring into mine. A fetid smell always helped me navigate my way to the creature.

Once I'd heard the tale of that first camp-out, I had to wonder: Did the baby I was look up and find those glowing green eyes watching her, smell the pungent breath from its mouth? If so, why would the creature have left her be, tender morsel that she was? Obviously, I'll never know for sure, except, perhaps, somewhere beyond conscious memory.

My first four years followed a culturally schizophrenic pattern, yet a pattern that felt perfectly normal to me. During the summers we spent in that canyon, I went barefoot on the rocky decomposed granite sand, clad only in cotton panties. When I wasn't running in the wash and along the low ridges, I was climbing piñon pines, picking acorns from scrub oak, or watching the dramas at anthills. I also liked to explore rocky outcrops for shady shelters where I could sit and imagine what might have happened there way back when Indians inhabited the land. Sometimes I caught and played with lizards or horned toads, spent hours chasing the bright blue, green and red dragonflies that came to the spring to drink and feed. (I never did catch one of those elusive creatures.) The wild plants and creatures became my companions. The only vestiges of civilization were those we brought ourselves – our tent and cots, the cooler hung from the piñon, the pots and pans mother used to cook with on the campfire. Visitors were rare, usually neighbors – which meant anyone who lived in a twenty-mile radius.

Summer days there were filled with wonders. I remember waking on my cot under the piñon at the first hum of dawn wind high on the mountains, remember watching the morning sun crest the ridge to shimmer from pine needles on the dancing branches overhead. In late spring the pine-scented air was also perfumed with the mixed scents of lupine, deep blue Canterbury Bells and orchid-like desert willow flowers. Manzanita blossoms, too, that looked like tiny pink lanterns. The aroma of mother's coffee on the campfire would soon mix with the rest, on good days joined by bacon and other yummy breakfast smells.

Getting up did not mean putting on shoes and socks and uncomfortable clothes, but simply putting on a clean pair of panties for the day. After breakfast, the morning would open its huge doors, and I would be free to partake of and interact with its infinite wonders. My favorite running ground until my feet toughened up each year was, of course, the wash where the granite sand was soft and friendly to bare feet. The big sage that grew there was soft, too, though its pungent scent was not. I loved making rings around those plants with white rocks, unknowingly following a tradition started by Bobette many years before. I made rings around the other plants as well, even the cholla cactus with its yellow blossoms, and the Spanish Dagger, whose fallen pods held big black seeds I liked to plant, though I often paid for that in blood if I was not careful.

Much of the day I spent making up stories where plants served characters. Lizards and insects – especially the long shiny green bugs that liked the lupine-and horned toads played their roles, too. If I were lucky enough to catch one, all the better. The horned toads were easiest to catch, though, and would stay around if I petted their heads to put them in a trance.

During winters in the city, we lived in a middle-class neighborhood with a green lawn. The plants that grew there were not scrubby and wild like sage and juniper and scrub oak, but lush and carefully trimmed. In the wild, flowers that came up on their own in the spring soon became dried shells of themselves. In Hollywood, flowers got watered and sprayed and many stayed around most of the year. During the day, I played with neighborhood friends in fenced yards or on concrete driveways, wore confining shoes and uncomfortable dresses. This dual life continued until we finally moved to the canyon full-time a year after my sister Carolyn was born. I was nearly five.

I did enjoy having human playmates when we were in the city and there were other good things about life in Hollywood, too, especially the Good Humor truck that came through the neighborhood clanging its bells each day. I recall one day when I was three that mother refused to buy me the ice cream treat she had promised. God had told her, she said, how I had taught the other neighborhood children to take off their shoes and walk around on the dirt that morning in the vacant lot around the corner, then how to go pee behind the bushes there – the way we always did when we lived in the canyon. I loved to go to that vacant lot, especially loved the rainbow-colored caterpillars on the wild fennel plants there. As crushed as I was about not getting my ice cream, I remember being even more puzzled about the method God had used to tell on me. Did he come to the front door. Did he call Mother on the phone? Mother refused to discuss the matter.

Yet, from the start, the wild was what took in me. Even in my city life I had stayed as close to wild as I could get. In Hollywood, when neighborhood kids came over for my fourth birthday party, along with a few of my mother's friends, we had ice cream and cake, of course, and played games. But the whole time I was squirming around in my scratchy organdy dress and the stiff patent-leather shoes hurt my feet. After the other kids left, I wanted to take off my party clothes, but the dress was buttoned up the back, and Mother and her friends were too busy talking and drinking coffee. She told me to go play with my new presents in my room until Daddy got home.

But those tight, scratchy birthday clothes kept driving me crazy. I must have kept tugging so hard at the collar of my dress that a button finally popped off, then another. I vaguely recall pulling the dress up over my head and the opening getting caught on my ears, struggling to get it off. I was afraid my ears would come with it, but I just had to get that dress off. I don't remember the details of the struggle to free my feet, but I do remember the release of freeing them from their patent-leather prisons and standing barefoot on the carpet, wiggling my toes with its softness.

Then I was out the door, running and running across the soft grass, then down the sidewalk toward the vacant lot. I don't remember why I stopped at the storm drain and flung my new ruby ring into the dark hole for good measure. I continued down the hard concrete sidewalk again, my feet yearning for soft wash sand of the canyon, but settling for the dirt of the vacant lot, a kind of powdery dirt, not the same as the granite sand of the canyon, but still dirt under my feet.

I hid myself among the tall fennel plants and peeked back through the soft, feathery branches to make sure that no one was coming after me. I knew I'd done bad but didn't feel bad. I extracted a few caterpillars from the anise plants and put them down around me to have another pretend birthday party.

I don't know how long it was before I heard my Daddy's

and Mother's voices calling my name in the distance. I scooted deeper into the fennel grove, the plants' brush-like leaves soft against my naked skin.

Of course, they found me. Mother glared at me with that mean look she always had in my dreams, but Daddy picked me up and carried me toward home. "What happened to your new birthday ring?" Mother wanted to know. I was afraid to tell her, but when Daddy asked I pointed back to the storm drain. Mother looked like she was going to slap me, but Daddy was there so she didn't. We went to the storm drain and both of them climbed down the metal ladder onto the platform above the dark drain itself. They kept asking and asking where I put the ring. Finally, they came up and took me home, then sent me to my room, while Daddy went back to try to find the birthday ring. By now I did feel bad and hoped they'd find it, but they never did.

I spent the rest of the day shut up alone in my room. At first I could hear them arguing. Mother wanted to take my new toys away but Daddy said no. I lay down on my bed and watched animals and people from my books playing on the walls and ceiling of my room like they always did when I was alone in there.

For that same birthday, Uncle Kit had also built me a sweet eight-by-eight playhouse. It was the perfect place to put rainbow caterpillars from the vacant lot to see if they would become butterflies like Daddy said they would. It seemed like a good place for the sow bugs and earthworms I found around the yard, too, especially for Lady Bugs, lots and lots of Lady Bugs. And soon after my birthday I thought it would be a good place for a wharf rat that I chased down into that big storm drain, cornering it on a metal platform. I didn't know it was a rat; I just knew I had to have this weird looking animal for my new playhouse. The rat jumped out at me when I tried to catch it, caught hold of my thumb with its huge rat teeth. It didn't behave at all like the squirrel I'd caught by the tail in the canyon. Somehow I must have gotten back up the steps because I remember running home with this rodent attached to my thumb. My father strangled the poor thing to get it off me.

Those years before I turned four, I had first two, then three, imaginary friends. Moo Moo, Gaa Gaa, and Lois with scary red eyes. Most of this I learned later from Mother and Bobette – though I do remember those little phantom friends vaguely, mainly from what seem to be dreamscapes, where we ran down tunnels into a magical underground world. They were baby-shaped creatures who always ran around in blue panties. I'm told I only had them around during those months we stayed in Hollywood, and apparently they disappeared around the time my sister was born.

~

In an odd way, Hollywood followed us back into the homestead canyon when we moved there year-round. Or, more accurately, we followed Hollywood back to the homestead – because the only reason we were able to move back to the homestead full-time was because Hollywood was building a faux Western town named Pioneertown about ten miles from our homestead. It was 1946, and the town was built to be the backdrop for western movies and for weekly television shows that were soon to become the rage. My father had hired on as a painter to "age" the new buildings so they would appear more like actual frontier town buildings. Naturally the place was and is named Pioneertown.

Over the next few flush years, we progressed from hauling water piped from the spring on the mountain to the bottom of the wash across from our tent, to having it piped it right down to our new cabin. I say cabin, but at first it was just another army tent around which my father and Uncle Kit eventually built wooden walls. Except, from the start the tent had one difference, a foundation and a floor with wooden planks. My mother had spent hours a day carting up rocks from the wash in a wheelbarrow to bringing the foundation up off the ground.

I remember helping by putting the smaller rocks into the wheelbarrow. Along with the wooden walls, my dad and Uncle Kit also built a small kitchen they attached to the walled tent with a passageway. Finally, one day a passel of 'neighbors' from around the area arrived for a roof-raising, followed by campfire dinner, with beer for the grownups and bottles of Coke for us kids. The event lasted late into the night.

Our new kitchen had a sink and a real butane stove, instead of the old woodstove, Cookie. Cookie was exiled to the yard though we still used her out there during the summer, spring and fall. Most summer meals were cooked on a simple campfire in our yard. That saved propane – and money. The campfire worked fine for simple meals like roasted hot dogs and grilled burgers we bought from a store in Yucca Valley, and for fried cottontail that Mother had shot, and for heating canned stews. We used Cookie for goat or venison stews, chili beans, small roasts, cobblers, biscuits and sometimes breakfast pancakes.

We slept outside in summers, too, under the billions of stars only be seen in such dark skies as our canyon had. Mother pointed out the bear constellations, *Ursa Major* and *Minor*. I found coyotes and mountain lions and rabbits in those skies, too, and many other creatures from the canyon as I lay awake in wonder. On the nights that moonlight drowned out all but the brightest stars, I woke often and followed its course between the canyon's mountains.

I attended first to third grades in a one-room schoolhouse that a few times became part of a movie set. On those days, all sixteen of us in grades one to six had to dress in funny clothes and become a backdrop for some scene that was being shot next to us. Once or twice the film crew even came inside, which was the only time we got to have real ink jars in the holes on our desks.

Without ever having seen a movie or TV show, I watched them being made while I waited in town to go home after school: Annie Oakley (played by Gail Davis in the TV series they were shooting), Gene Autry, Roy Rogers, and Cisco Kid were the regulars. I can remember sitting on Roy Rogers' lap in the Golden Stallion, a Chinese Restaurant the movie folks built and frequented. I once had a picture of myself on Gene Autry's horse, Champion, though no memory of Autry lifting me up on his horse so my father could take a picture of me there. I considered these movie men quite nice, but I thought they were really silly to wear so much make-up. None of the real cowboys I knew dressed like that, wore make-up or smelled like perfume; real cowboys wore wrinkly hats and shirts and smelled like sweat and manure.

Watching movies being made could be quite tiresome. I remember swinging on the porch rail of the Red Dog Saloon as "Annie Oakley" rode up, dismounted and stuck a gun in the back of a man dressed in black. Cut. I watched her do it again and again until the director was satisfied. Watched stiffly dressed cowboys in make-up have fake fist fights with Gene Autry and Roy Rogers, over and over and over, while phony pops accompanied their near-miss fisticuffs. I watched until I got bored, then went off to chase lizards and find beer bottles to cash in for two cents apiece so I could fill my ever-hungry tummy with peanuts from the little coin-operated machine.

I hadn't yet been exposed to the results – the seduction of the "silver screen." Our new cabin, as up-graded as it was, never did have electricity. It was miles too far from the nearest small town, and only ourselves and the miners lived in the canyon full-time. But we prided ourselves in being real homesteaders who shot a lot of the meat we ate, and grew vegetables in a garden. Butane was plenty civilized enough for us.

Much later, when I was around thirteen, I would be seduced by a certain movie, *Rebel Without a Cause*, an event which powerfully affected my life. Ironic as it seems to me now, I didn't make any connection between it and the faked fight scenes I'd watched. Now that I think about it, I *had* seen one film as a young child – and that one, I think, also had a huge impact on my life. It was a short documentary about plants and photosynthesis at Bobette's wedding in Hollywood, just before I turned four. I was one of several children being cared for in a back room of the Hollywood Presbyterian Church, and I remember being fascinated as I watched the depiction of how plants take in food and water from their roots and transform it with photosynthesis. I can still picture the food being carried up the plant's branches on what looked like small railroad cars. That little film managed to affect me deeply and left me with a profound respect for plant life. It showed me that plants were living beings just as people are. I was and continue to be awed by the miraculous process hidden in even the most ordinary-looking plant. As a young girl, I continued to sing out my love to the canyon's many plants. If I sang my songs too close to the cabin, though, or while we were riding to school in the jeep, Mother would tell me to "stop those damn mouth noises." Then I would continue to sing silently to them.

Before I was old enough to read books and learn more about plants and the rest of the wild around me, I picked up what I could here and there, mostly from observation. I learned, too, from my grandmother, who visited us occasionally, that many "weeds" could be eaten. There were lamb's quarters, pepper plants, pigweed, and purslane. Other plants, like yerba santa and ephedra, were actually medicines that we sometimes made into tea when we were ill. Manzanita berries were edible too, as were the seeds of the desert almond bushes. Even Mother always took us to gather piñon nuts to roast and eat. Acorns from the scrub oaks around us never made the grade.

I was told by Indian George, a Serrano Indian who lived four miles down canyon with John Olsen and the Swedish miners, that acorns, along with many other things, were ground up and eaten by his people. The bitterness had to be rinsed out first, George said. Of course, he didn't tell me that the scrub-oak acorns were only used in starvation times when the larger acorns from big black oaks (and had much less bitter tannin) weren't available. I spent countless impossible hours trying to soak and rinse out the tannic acid from shrub oak acorns. Then I would smash them up with a rock and make them into the bitterest sundried bread imaginable. Absolutely inedible. Especially since, not knowing any better, I always soaked and rinsed the acorns in their shells, rather than after they were shelled and ground, the way people who knew what they were doing would have done. Even soaking them without shells would have made that shrub oak acorn flour a bit less bitter, although the best way would have been to rinse them after they were ground to flour.

I became fascinated by the idea that not long ago Indian George's people lived entirely from the wild land and plants and animals around them. Food from desert plants and animals was sparse and must have taken an incredible amount of work and knowledge, I realized. It seemed heroic. No one brought supplies to them on weekends, and they had no matches to start their cooking fires, he told me. And the mysterious and musical sounds of the language he and his friends spoke among themselves seemed to come directly from the wild land around me that I loved. The few glimpses he showed me of his culture and ceremonies also felt like part of that land. I spent hours and hours dreaming about what that world must have been like, acting out what I imagined in daily dramas.

I loved animals too, even the ones we ate. I could hardly wait until I was old enough to shoot the rabbits we fried up for dinner. I loved to watch mother peel down the skin of rabbits hung from our clothesline, pulling it off like a pair of pajamas before she slit open the balloon of belly. I relished the pretty designs and colors of intestines, though I wasn't as fond of the pungent smell. Deer and young goats had the same fate on our homestead, and I watched them being skinned with equal fascination. Were their eye balls hard? Could they be rolled like marbles, I wondered? I was never to be fooled by the pretty packages of meat in supermarkets.

Life in the canyon now included having a grey pony of my own named Sox, and that pony never stopped running away with me – one time dragging me miles with my foot caught in the stirrup – and bucking me off every other time I rode him. Sox, though, was only a pale imitation of another pony I sometimes saw hanging around the water at the Willows down canyon, where John Olsen and the Swedes squatted. This was the horse I really loved. This horse-of-my-dreams was a deep blue gray roan, was slimmer and more shapely. And it ran wild. Sox seemed like everything else I came across in the "civilized" world, only a faded imitation of the world of my imagination. Everything disappointed, except things that were wild. Wild seemed like the only true thing I could count on.

Chapter Four
1950
Someone Smarter Than I Am in There

Just before I turned nine, my father managed to drag Mother out of her canyon to live in the city again. Once the building-boom to create Pioneertown ended, it became impossible for him to make a living in the desert. If she hadn't had three children under age nine and one of them a toddler, Mother most likely would have much preferred for him to live and work in the L.A. area and come up bringing groceries every couple weeks or so. That was her old *Modes Operandi*: she would have had her life intact, have her freedom and groceries to eat, too, you might say. But her changed situation had made her agree to come with him to live in what she called "the city," which in reality turned out to be a rural/farming town called Bassett, about thirty miles east of Los Angeles proper. Places like the Bassett of 1950 don't exist near L.A. today – if they exist anywhere at all. This time we stayed in the city quite a while, although we returned to stay in the canyon each summer until I was nearly twelve, at which time Mother did move back with the three of us children.

The rural area, even with its farms and dairies – I used to walk up the street to the original Alta Dena dairy daily for bottles of fresh milk – and fields of various vegetables, felt profoundly urban to us after living in the wilderness. There was Crawford's huge grocery store only five miles away in El Monte, a more sizable town with several department stores, a theater and all paved roads. Everyone in the city had telephones (our phone number was 62440) and electricity, and most people lived in little tract houses with lawns and fences. It was a long way away from the wild canyon I knew. It was a big jump, too, going from a one-room schoolhouse with sixteen students total to a school where there were twenty-five or more in each grade. From a school where I wore mostly jeans and cowboy boots, to a school that required girls to wear dresses and fancy-pants shoes. And from a school where I knew everyone, to one where there were hundreds of kids I did not know at all.

I remember being bullied on the playground at the new school by three older Mexican girls that I kept following around the schoolyard. We didn't have Mexicans in our little desert community, and maybe I was paying so much attention to them because I loved hearing the sounds of the Spanish they spoke among themselves on the playground. The sound of Spanish was so musical – and so unlike English or even the clipped and harsh sounds of the desert Indian languages, Serrano, Cahuilla and Chemuhuevi that I had heard from Indian George and his friends. For whatever reason, the girls began to taunt me, talking in Spanish to each other in ways that made it clear they were making fun of me. Somehow I could understand words like *"estupida"* and others that sounded enough like English I could make out the meaning. And the tone and intent were unmistakable.

After a couple days of this, I turned around and spoke to them in Apache. At least that's what I told them it was. Of course, I was only imitating the rhythms and inflections of the desert Indians, but I chose to call myself Apache because I knew Apaches were the bad asses of western Indians. I'd learned that much from hearing the dialogue of the faux cowboys shooting movies in Frontiertown.

Of course, the girls didn't believe for a minute that this little blond newcomer was really an Apache Indian. Although they must have been far closer to being Apache than I was, they had probably only seen Apaches in the same movies that I had watched being made. But they had no way to disprove it, and I was pretty convincing with the sound aspects. My memory was good enough that I could remember some of the "words" and phrases I made up, and I would reuse them convincingly. After a few days, the girls gave up and left me alone – and I left them alone.

Back at our new little tract home, I'd found enough wildish places outside the streets of box houses to feel somewhat at home – fallow fields, open hills behind the railroad tracks, and a dry riverbed. Each weekend I dragged my now almost six-year-old sister Carolyn, and later, once he turned three, my brother Danny, off to the hills with me to hunt gopher snakes and catch lizards and insects to play with. Even though these places were only pale imitations of the real wild I knew, at least they were something.

Soon we even had a TV. In our canyon, we'd had a battery radio, with a long wire antenna that ended wrapped around a piñon branch up on the mountain. I got to hear all the good shows my mother listened to in the evening, like *Lux Radio Theater*, *Fibber McGee and Molly*, and the *Lone Ranger*. In the city, Mother let me watch only kid shows like *Beanie and Cecil*. After a couple TV kid shows, we were put to bed each night. But I'd convinced Dad that I'd become afraid of the dark, so he would leave the door open a crack. It was through this crack that I saw the "real" grownup stories; *One Million Years B.C.* was my favorite. I also got to see the late news, too, and then hear my parents talk about the evil Russians, who were the cause of us sometimes having to hide under our desks at school. The United States of America and our President Ike were the good guys, and Khrushchev was the president of those evil people.

Around that time I became concerned, maybe even obsessed, about good and evil in general, what evil was and what it meant and how it related to what I was learning in Sunday school. Then one day in Sunday school, a powerful thought took hold of me. It occurred to me in one big flash that God and the Devil were really just symbols (though I didn't know the word, I had the concept down cold) of good and evil and not actual beings at all. And maybe these things, God, Satan, Good, Evil, weren't any more real than Santa Claus and the Easter Bunny. I could hardly wait to get home and share my great insight.

Well, when I got home and explained my new idea to Mother, who was the only one home at the time, I found she did not share my excitement at the discovery. She, in fact, slapped me so hard I flew back and banged my head on the wall. "That's blasphemy," hissed this woman who would later brag to me about her own religious searches when she was a young woman. But she never made that connection. Like most people, Mother had her share of cognitive dissonance, a concept I learned later from psychology books, and I know she probably only knocked the daylights out of me trying to save me from going to hell.

Mother's tendency toward cognitive dissonance/hypocrisy, or whatever it was, seemed more pronounced whenever we lived in the city. Around the time I made my discovery, Mother had managed to become president of the local PTA and was working to found a center for teen activities. Meanwhile, we, her own children, were taking the brunt of some of her craziest episodes. Maybe living in the city was driving her crazy or something; she was having migraines as well. The violent episodes took place only at home in private and seemed to have no effect on her public persona. A week or two after my revelation, I remember her pulling a sliding door out from the closet and trying to slam it against my little sister for sleeping with our cat hidden in her bed. Then she went in and shoved three-year-old Danny's head into the toilet and tried to flush him down – he had wet the bed, which he continued to do in stressful times up until the affair with his Sunday school teacher when he was fifteen. (That sure cured him in a hurry.)

I pulled Mother away from Danny, saying that PTA presidents weren't supposed to be hurting their children like that. Naturally that turned her rage onto me. I didn't get the closet door or big flush treatment. Instead, she grabbed her usual weapon, the old ironing cord, and whipped me until my legs and arms were bloody and full of welts. My body too. It wasn't the first time. Some part of me wondered how many other presidents of PTAs were doing those kinds of things.

To be fair, I can point to some behaviors on her part that were just as dissonant when we lived in the canyon, where we continued to spend summers even while we lived in the city, as well as during the four-hour trip there for weekends in fall and spring. I just don't remember her being as physically violent as she was while we lived in the city.

I should probably say something here, too, about the lineage of powerful and somewhat crazy women that was and is a part of our family. I knew only a little of this history at the time but have tried as an adult to piece together the bigger picture from stories I heard from family members and from interrogations I made of other family members, sometimes with sparse results. We all called my mother's mother Kee Kee, a name she gave herself that came from Mexican slang for breasts, although she claimed the nickname was French. Most of the history I have about her came from Mother, who certainly had a negative bias. Mother claimed Kee Kee always had men in her bed when Mother's father was at work. Apparently that was quite often since he owned a bar in Juarez, across the Mexican border from their El Paso home. Mother's maiden name was Arnold and, according to her, her father, James Arnold, was a direct descendent of Benedict Arnold's brother. (An uncle's genealogy later backed that up.) That was one family secret. The other secret was the so-called "Indian blood" that came from Kee Kee's mother (or it could have been her grandmother), who, according to that same uncle, was a true mad woman who used to beat soundly all of her nine children daily.

Mother got beat too, though not by Kee Kee, who merely kept score of Mother's trespasses, then turned the information over to one of her Mexican housekeepers and ordered her to do it – one blow of the strap for each offence. And Mother, who went through her childhood largely unsupervised, always had

49

many offences. Kee Kee had four more marriages after James Arnold died young – as did every other of her new husbands, eventually. Mother implied that the deaths involved Kee Kee's cooking and knowledge of herbs. According to Mother, at one point Kee Kee served as a madam and operated a "rest home" where she devoted one wing to that more dubious occupation. She had been hired at the rest home after claiming to have been supervisor at a rest home that had burned to the ground in a Kansas City.

I knew Kee Kee myself first as a henna-haired woman who occasionally came to live with us for short spurts, which would always end with her and Mother rolling around on the floor trying to pull out each other's hair. In her later years, she became more grey-haired-grandmotherly and even religious, although she had another side to her that allowed her to earn money supplemental to her social security by holding tarot readings in her apartment.

During one of the times she stayed with us, however, I got a peek at her true self – or at least her dark side. This didn't happen until I was fourteen and we had again returned to the city after another two year stay in the desert. By this time I was a high school freshman. Each day when I came home from school, I did the dishes, vacuumed and did the other housework Mother required of me. Kee Kee would follow me around as I did the chores, telling me how unfair she thought it was that Mother would make a girl my age do all the housework. "She treats you like a slave," she told me over and over. That was a new perspective for me, but it didn't take long before I began feeling very put upon by this "slavelike" treatment.

Then one day school let out early, and I came home and overheard her in the den telling Mother what a lazy spoiled brat I was. She told Mother that she needed to make her lazy daughter do more housework and take on more responsibilities. I rushed into the den and confronted her, telling mother what Kee Kee had been saying to me. There followed another floor-rolling hair-pull and Kee Kee left the next day. Although I hated to have caused the altercation, I was glad to get that witch out of our house.

I have never fully understood what would make someone engage – a grandmother, mind you – in such behavior toward her own family. She had spent hours getting into my confidence, as I'm sure she had mother's, then focused on what she saw as a weak spot and used it to damage our family. I am just grateful that I came home early and overheard her – otherwise I would never have caught a glimpse into that particular family dynamic.

(Just recently, I learned that Kee Kee had fully instructed my brother as a teenager on just how to set off family conflict bombs, and demonstrated doing so at a Thanksgiving dinner.)

The story of Kee Kee's character stands in stark contrast to character of another powerful woman in our family, Cally, Kee Kee's elder sister, who was head of the women's division of the El Paso police force. The story of her character I have found corroborated in books about El Paso history, where sometimes several pages were devoted to her. Apparently, she was known for checking on and protecting the many prostitutes working in El Paso, and was widely revered for sending many of the very young ones back home with money out of her own pocket.

Like Mother, Kee Kee and myself, Cally stood just under five foot tall. Yet once in ten-year-old Bobette's presence Cally managed to plunk a six-foot-tall robber onto the floor of the grocery story he was robbing (they'd been standing in line behind him). With one foot on his neck and her gun pointed at his head, according to Bobette, she then said, "I wouldn't do that if I was you, sonny."

Even this remarkable female relative, however, was not completely heroic. Bobette also recounts stories of the time when she lived with that part of the family when she saw the heroic police woman come home and chase her daughters through the house, sometimes over and across their beds, swinging her husband's big belt, and never stopping until she achieved her goal of beating them "within an inch" of their lives. As powerfully heroic as she was, as with the other women in my family, she expressed herself efficiently with violence.

I think now that I learned early to detach myself from the violence perpetrated by the powerful women in our family, especially Mother. I observed and intellectualized things that otherwise might have been horrific. It enabled me to not get caught up in seeing myself as a victim of behaviors that I somehow understood had little to do with me. Otherwise I never would have survived. When the scene plays in my head now of the PTA president's violence, I can vaguely remember Danny and Carolyn screaming and sobbing. I can better recall the focused fury of my mother as madwoman, can still hear the hissed breath, smell the angry sweat that came with her face distorted by and anger and evil intent. I remember nothing about the terror I must have felt – maybe because it was such an old and familiar danger, one I always knew might manifest at any moment. Only my detached observations have stayed with me.

I experienced that terror more directly from another recurring dream I'd had since I was tiny. The dream went like this: I'm tied to some railroad tracks, and a huge locomotive is barreling down on me. It's one of those old black locomotives with dark steam rising above it. My mother and father are somehow standing on the front of this train, like icons on an old ship. Mother is glaring straight down at me, her face contorted into a menacing grimace. And my father? Well, he's looking off into the distance and smiling. In my terror, I realize he will never look down and save me from her. My dreams always got straight to the heart of the matter.

I'm sure at some point I experienced that terror when subject to Mother's rages, even if I don't remember it. I must have learned early not to take her attacks personally, any more than I did those of a pet gopher snake that once bit me when I picked it up, or the earthquake that knocked my porcelain palomino from the shelf and broke it. I don't know quite how that attitude came about, but it was crucial to surviving. Even as I look back at it, I still don't think her rage was meant to break any of us – and it didn't. She was more like a mother bear or jackal, batting her young around in moments of frustration. It was a toughening experience in some ways, as long as we survived it.

Besides, my mother had given me a powerful, almost magical gift. She had drummed it into me during her good periods that I could do and be anything at all I set my mind to. Even then, I recognized that surviving her rages was good evidence of that. And although her own life had left its mark on her, Mother had certainly retained her power. I had understood for some time that I was smarter and stronger than she was (other than physically). This sense of my own power that kept me from collapsing also kept me from realizing that I wasn't strong enough to escape her effects completely. Today my legs and body show no trace of the bloody stripes she left, though I'm sure they must still exist somewhere inside where no one can see them.

It's funny the things I do remember, though – and what my current viewpoint adds them memory. What is fascinating about those things for me is that they stay with me for mysterious reasons, all of them holding troves of things I needed to understand about myself. As if someone smarter than me was inside saving them until I was ready to understand them.

A case in point: I remember being out in the driveway watering irises alongside our house in Bassett, during the same era my mother was the PTA president. I was obsessing about good and evil again, thinking about how Khrushchev wanted to bomb us, but wondering if he really was the evil man everyone said, the man who wanted to kill the children in our country.

What if he thought we wanted to kill the children in his country, I wondered? Maybe all the talk of evil was just a misunderstanding between the two countries. I'd heard a bit of Russian spoken on the TV news, and it seemed pretty impossible to understand; a lot harder than the Spanish those girls spoke. It seemed likely to me at the time that a lot could be misunderstood between the two languages. If the leaders could just sit down and talk to each other, maybe things could be worked out without the terrible bombs. I wished I spoke Russian so I could try to explain to Khrushchev that neither of us were the evil ones, that our countries were just afraid of each other.

This time I knew better than to ask Mother or Dad what they thought. I suspected it was another kind of blasphemy.

But this is the keeper from that scene, what I *also* remember: All the while I was having these profound thoughts about the nature of good and evil and doubting that evil was any more than a misunderstanding. I remember clearly the evil I was perpetrating myself, which was plucking snails from my mother's irises that grew beside the driveway, carefully turning each snail over and pouring salt on it, then watching with delight as their soft insides dissolved into a mass of foam. This horrific action was officially sanctioned by my parents. After all these snails *were* the bad guys who ate the irises. Nothing in me then made any connection between the evil I was trying to understand and the evil I was gleefully committing on those poor snails as I contemplated evil in the abstract. Nothing conscious, that is. But something in me must have watching or I would never have hung on to that part of the memory.

So I remembered it later and understood the irony, which is why I have come to suspect that we all have someone or something smarter inside ourselves that decides what and when we understand our own inner workings – in this case my own lack of self-reflection and cognitive disassociation. Maybe some part of us is trying to help the everyday us understand things. Although we see only what we are capable of seeing at the time, that smarter, more aware part of us in our unconscious tries to show us a different picture when we can bear to look at what our conscious mind, with its ego and self-image concerns, refuses to see. Why else would these kinds of memories persist until we get their message? I have countless other memories that demonstrate that latent-memory phenomenon.

This certainly isn't the repressive unconscious of Freud, which has an opposite purpose that is just as real. This is more like the unconscious of C. J. Jung, someone I was delighted to discover when reading through the psychologists soon after the experience with the run-over dog when I was twenty-three. Jung's unconscious is full of mystery and hopeful belief that some kind of core purpose inside directs our unfolding. Something called the Jungian Self, which can be individual and/or collective. I have come to believe that this self-director shows us our own darknesses when we're ready, rather than repressing or hiding them from us. It's still up to each of us to acknowledge our own darkness, and many of us refuse to look at it. Because of that refusal, we instead project our own darkness onto other people and cultures. Only if we do acknowledge it will we cease to be driven by it and cease using and wasting our energy trying to keep it out of our sight and projected firmly onto those "others" who are the "real" bad guys!

Chapter Five
1965
Searching for Answers

Not long after I shot that suffering dog back in 1965, Daryl's hallucinations became so severe that I realized he was not just making plays for attention. There were no options for psychiatric treatment anywhere in the high desert where we lived, and the culture there I'd been raised in didn't even recognize the need for such a thing. I immediately dived deep into books by Freud, Adler and every other psychologist and psychiatrist I could get my hands on in the library. It didn't take long for me to realize that Daryl needed more help than theories, so I found in another kind of book, a phone book, a psychiatrist in San Bernardino, seventy miles away. He put Daryl on Stelazine. That calmed things down some, but only for a short while.

Truth be told, I was going a little crazy myself around this time. A few months before, I had read Simone de Beauvoir's *The Second Sex*, which had a much more immediate and dramatic effect on me than anything I had read thus far. The French philosopher's passionate but scholarly and thorough historical deconstruction of the role of women in Western culture nailed me to the wall. I now understood how the human race had defined the male as the quintessential human being. According to de Beauvoir, this made the female merely a secondary "other," and that this was true in the conscious and unconscious thinking of women as well as men, causing us to passively accept this secondary role. The idea exposed me for what I was at age twenty-three with five children, right down to my long and, by then, platinum hair.

De Beauvoir's irrefutable argument explained why my eighth grade teacher had told me that it was 'too bad so much intelligence was wasted on a girl,' why my seventh grade teacher had tried to pawn me off to tutor her pet, Billy Smith, just because he had a crush on me, why the counselor during my one year of high school had guided me toward nursing or teaching – both of which I hated at the time – when I said I was more interested in science and languages, and why she told me it would be "too hard" for me to take both Spanish and French at the same time, even though I was getting all A's without trying (except in algebra, where I had to study my butt off to get the A). And de Beauvoir's book certainly explained why I insisted on strutting my curvy shape around town to get the approval of the "more powerful" gender. In short, I now understood the dynamic behind my having married such an untrustworthy member of the power gender, a man who lied habitually about where he had been, who he had seen, and why. For the first time I had an inkling of insight into the unconscious and conscious forces that had made me the mother of five by the time I was twenty-three.

At least that's how I saw it at the time. Other factors had contributed, too, of course, such as my own headstrong nature and being raised in the wild with a damaged but (thankfully) untamed mother, who had been caught in the same second sex gender trap without ever seeing or understanding it. But those things wouldn't occur to me for quite some time.

I'm sure my new insights weren't helping Daryl during his breakdown. During the previous months, I had changed from a raging atheist to a raging feminist. And I do mean raging. I didn't stop being an atheist either. I simply recognized the male dominance of the Biblical god figure that I'd already rejected for being such an ass in Old Testament stories. That wasn't very analytical nor philosophically sound, nor even a permanent conclusion, but it was my gut reaction at the time.

Soon after reading de Beauvoir, I went back to being 'natural.' I cut and dyed my hair back to something like it had become beneath the platinum. If guys didn't like me that way, tough. Of course, going natural didn't cost that much in terms of male admiration at age twenty-three. I'd never worn makeup in the first place, but now it was not worn on principle. And my principles were suddenly ferocious. God, so to speak, help any man who so much as opened a door for me.

Meanwhile, I continued my rampage through book after book, which now included the psychologists. I can't say that I always understood everything I read in the hundreds of books I'd plowed through in my quest for answers, but I did know an answer when one finally hit me between the eyeballs. I think that after reading the Bible at age seventeen, I had stopped looking for answers directly and simply got caught up in the reading quest itself. After my exposure to the other book about historical context of the Old Testament, I continued to read for insights, but with a critical eye to each author's own ego, agendas and cultural/social thinking of (usually) his era. Oh, there were answers of sorts everywhere, but, although I couldn't have articulated it then, I had realized by this time that what the books contained was a dialogue on human life, with everyone sounding in with his (and rarely her) own culturally and ideologically tainted view on things.

But Simone de Beauvoir's book transcended all that – in fact, it included all that in its conclusions. Her ideas provided an Answer with a capital A. She spoke a Truth that had affected the whole of my life, a Truth I could see at work in every day, in every hour of my life – and in the lives of everyone I knew. If Sartre took over a thousand pages to tell us abstrusely how we only truly exist to the extent we create ourselves out of conscious choices (choices I wasn't sure I believed were consciously made in the first place), his friend, lover and fellow philosopher, de Beauvoir, took a few less pages to show clearly just how forces outside of ourselves create who we become without our being conscious of it. That was more true to the rough, rut road of my own life experience.

I became obsessed with sharing my new insights about the way women had been conditioned to be "second," even (or especially) in their own minds, to anyone I could force to listen to me. I had seen the light, and the world was my congregation to convert. Naturally, this included Daryl. He wasn't the only one who didn't want to hear it. When at a Thanksgiving dinner, I applied my new insights to certain Biblical pronouncements on women's role, my father came across the living room toward me with violence in his eyes – the only time he ever came close to doing such a thing. Luckily, he tripped over the footstool of a chair and fell flat onto the floor. The surge of victory I felt didn't stop me from getting out of there before he got to his feet.

Even my sister Bobette, who had gone back to college in her thirties and garnered a B.A. in English – and who had been the only one I could have a decent conversation with about Shakespeare, Tolstoy or Dostoevsky – actually stopped speaking to me for a year after I tried to preach to her about de Beauvoir's ideas. In Bobette's view, the only reason I believed de Beauvoir's false ideas was because I was trying to get out of the responsibility for "ending up" the way I had. The big wave of American feminism and Betty Friedan's new book hadn't yet washed over American culture, so no one was about to take seriously anything a pipsqueak high school dropout with five kids had to say. That didn't stop me from trying.

Okay, so I now had some kind of answer – if not the answer to life itself, at least it was a big clue to how I ended up with *my* life. The forces that had shaped me seemed clear enough. What wasn't at all clear was what I could do about it at this point. Daryl continued to have psychotic episodes (which sent me even deeper into Freud, Adler, Horney, etc., and finally led me to Jung), and he was sneaking off from jobs and stealing things from the houses he painted so that even my father was about to fire him; I was still a twenty-five-year-old high school dropout who worked as waitress to support five kids under the age of seven; and we were still dirt poor with one station wagon coughing along on two cylinders. If I'd assessed the situation intellectually, I could have easily seen that it would be impossible to ever get out of it. Luckily, such an assessment was not my *modus operandi*, at least not a conscious assessment – and the unconscious knows better than to believe in logic. Even today, I'm not convinced that conscious choices are what matter – or rather that most of the choices we make are conscious and not merely rationales concocted by the consciousness to explain our unconscious motivations. It seems to me that our own underground forces are much more powerful and just fool us into thinking our choices are "conscious."

So while de Beauvoir had clued me in about how I got into my situation, it never occurred my conscious self to start planning ways of getting out of it, to look for ways of creating my being through conscious choices ala Sartre. (Besides, who wants a passel of imaginary crab companions following one around, the way they had poor Sartre?) Moreover, Freud, Adler, Horney, Jung and the rest of the psychological theorists I read to find answers for Daryl's psychosis were also giving me glimpses into other dynamics that were directing my own behavior, and those ideas seemed much more relevant. I could recognize complex after complex in myself and was only comforted by the fact that every psychologist I read seemed to have a different view of the significance of each complex; therefore, maybe they weren't the quite authorities each claimed to be. Maybe, I reasoned, what they described were dynamics of everyone's psyche and were only something to worry about if they got out of control – as with Daryl and Mother – and affected their daily behavior. I, myself, had nothing to worry about, right?

Reading Freud *did* help me to understand an incident with silverware and ashtrays that occurred when I was in the first grade. It was another memory that had stayed with me in that Jungian sort of way, though the dynamic of the incident was a dramatic demonstration of Freud's view of the unconscious. Somehow, both unconsciousnesses (Freud's and Jung's) were operating at the same time, in that I remembered the incident when I needed to.

The context for the memory was this: It was the summer after my first grade year in the one room schoolhouse in Frontiertown, and we were living in the new cabin Dad and Uncle Kit had built in the canyon from the wooden-walled tent. I had been chasing our big, mean goose away from my three-year-old little sister, when I tripped over a small clump of six-inch high spines that constitutes an infant Joshua tree. Though I was barely hurt I could not keep stop myself from crying. I started to sob wildly and kept on sobbing. I was truly inconsolable and just couldn't stop sobbing. It got so bad that Mother came running out of the cabin believing I must be really hurt. After she checked for broken bones and such and found none, she tried to comfort me – and I let her. Already two things are unusual about this incident. One is that things like falling, skinning knees, stubbing toes were just a part of my daily experience. I never cried over little things like that. Besides, I hadn't even hurt myself. The second strange thing is that I let Mother hold and comfort me, something I can only remember doing one other time later in my childhood when an eerie noise at night (that we found out later came from our new refrigerator) had me thinking space aliens were landing in our yard. My mother's arms had to be the least safe place I knew.

It didn't take long before Mother grew tired of comforting me. "You're not hurt, Susie," she said, holding me out from her. "You don't have a mark on you. What are you really crying about?" That's when things got even more strange. I remember that, even as the words left my lips, I was totally surprised at the story I blurted out about how I "stole" silverware and ashtrays.

Please bear with me; the backstory is this: After school a few months before, Monica, the only other first- grader, and I had walked through the Pioneertown dump in the dry wash behind the little town. (In those days, the custom of desert residents when disposing of unburnable refuse was to throw it into a wash to wait for the next flood to carry it away.) Since we lived so far from school, I often walked home with Monica and waited for one of my parents to show up. But on this particular day, Monica and I discovered a great treasure. Someone had thrown out a huge collection of old silverware, forks, knives, spoons, wooden bowls and several wooden serving spoons too. There was also a set of copper ashtrays, three in all, along with some wooden trays. Wow. What a find!

Even as we collected these treasures and took them to Monica's room at her house back in town, I couldn't help but feel guilty – as if we were stealing them. Logically, I knew better; after all, they had been in the dump. But these things were so wonderful that I had a hard time believing someone didn't want them. Maybe someone had accidentally set them in the dump and would return for them. That might have been why I told Monica that we could just keep them in her room for the time being and that I would take my share home after the weekend.

On the following Monday, though, Monica told me that her big brother and his friends had found our treasure and stolen it, taking it to their own hideout. Monica didn't want to let him get away with that and I agreed, so we crept into his hideout and took some of our treasure back. I took a set of silverware, a fork, a knife and spoon, and two of the ashtrays.

The guilt I felt for stealing these things from the dump in the first place was now compounded when we 're-stole' our treasure from her brother. Intellectually, I was still aware that I shouldn't be feeling guilty even as we perpetrated this act. Yet it had become a matter of principle now to get them away from Monica's brother. I gave away the things I took as quickly as I could – an ashtray to Indian George at the Swedes' place, an ashtray to my mother and the silverware to Aunt Ruth. Whew! Then I forgot all about the incident until several months later when I found myself blurting out my guilty story to Mother.

I don't remember exactly what came of all this at the time. I think Mother reassured me that I was in the clear. But I still remember my own shock as a six year old in hearing the words blurt out of my mouth and realized vaguely even then that I'd been harboring this guilty feeling – rational or not – until it festered inside and came pouring out like psychic green pus. It seemed a puzzle to mull over. It would be twenty years before I would discover an answer to that puzzle when I read about the repressive unconscious of Freud – and of the Jungian self waiting just below conscious awareness to teach us that we need to know about ourselves.

(And this isn't the end of the silverware story, either, though I won't bore you with excessive detail. Just enough to make my point about the power of the unconscious: When I was in my forties and working as a college instructor and director of a literary reading series, I stopped at a small restaurant with an internationally famous author whom I greatly admire and ordered hamburgers to go. When the receptionist behind the register accused me of putting silverware from the table into my purse, I immediately became a madwoman, emptying my purse and hamburgers-to-go sack on her glass countertop by the cash register, and telling her to put the hamburgers you-know-where. The huge receptionist came at me, and the famous writer had to jump in between us to stop us from tearing each other apart.

And, even after that was over, as I was driving back to the college, I still had to stop the car and pour out the contents of my purse to make sure I really hadn't stolen the silverware "again" without realizing it. The repressive Freudian unconscious is a powerful and completely irrational force. I *know* I didn't steal that silverware from the dump, or from any stupid restaurant. I'm not a notorious silverware thief. but something in me still doesn't quite *believe* it.

Anyway, back to life with Daryl. Not long after the dog incident in 1965 Daryl and I ended up moving to Pasadena, a sizable city on the outskirts of Los Angeles. The exact details of just how the move happened or why I can't remember clearly, other than Daryl got it in his mind that it was living in the desert and working for my father that was driving him crazy. Why did I go along with all this? Could it have been to leave the discomfort of living next to Sharon? Was I still worried that he'd find a way to slay whatever dragon he had her confused with? Or was my dad about to fire him? I really don't remember. Life with Daryl was always spiraling out of control. I do remember there had been several times when Daryl simply disappeared from jobs for hours at a time, sometimes coming in late at night with cockamamie stories about what had happened.

I remember, too, that one of Daryl's old friends had promised him a job in Pasadena that paid twice as much as my father paid him. At least that's what Daryl said. Maybe that's why I went along with it. Daryl also said that his psychologist told him that a change might be a good thing, though I'll never know if that was true either. So we shucked off our life and that little house we were buying as if it were any old rental. I didn't even cry as we drove off.

During most of the four months total we lived in Pasadena, Daryl worked days, and I worked nights as a waitress, leaving for work soon after Daryl got home and the kids were fed. I would return home around three in the morning, not long before the kids woke up. The job Daryl's friend had promised turned out to pay less, not more, than my father had paid him, and everything in the city was considerably more expensive. The hallucinations ramped up again and, after a brief period of complete denial, Daryl started seeing a psychologist in the area. The new psychologist encouraged him to consider hospitalization. At first Daryl wouldn't even entertain that option. Even I didn't realize how badly he needed hospitalization – perhaps because I was so whacked out myself most of the time from arriving home at 3:00 am and getting up with the kids two or three hours later at 5:00 or 6:00 am.

As I think back now, I can see that some odd things were

happening. I don't remember the context of the incident, but I do remember him coming at me, diabolically laughing, his two index fingers extended and pointed directly at my eyes. Although he was laughing, I certainly wasn't. I remember also finding, on two separate "nights off," the remnants of pills Daryl had put in my coffee. The first time it was a white lump that had to be Benzedrine – and just when I was hoping to finally get some sleep. The other time, I found what must have been a bluish lump of stelazine; I'd checked my empty coffee cup after spending hours with goose bumps that prickled unbearably all over my skin.

At one point I was worried enough to call Bobette, who came over and confronted Daryl about the pills he had been denying he gave me. After talking about his life for hours, he admitted that he'd done it and said he didn't know why.

During this time, I also contracted a mysterious case of "food poisoning" that no one else in the family got, one that lasted for several weeks. (There went my waitressing job.) I became violently ill one evening – it was another of my nights off – and couldn't even hold down water for days. The food poisoning went on for more days, then weeks, with little relief. It was three weeks before I could hold down even broth. I lost twenty-five pounds, and weighed in just under eighty pounds when it was over. Several days, into the illness I asked Daryl to call the emergency room and ask someone there if I should come in. He went out to make the call at a phone booth (we had no phone). When he returned, he claimed that the nurse there told him that I just had to wait for it to go away.

Strange that I didn't connect my food poisoning and his assertion that I just had to "wait for it to go away" to any of Daryl's psychotic behaviors. Clearly I must have been too weak and sick, or too naive, to think straight. It took forty years, and my writing about this, before I even wondered about it. Fortunately, four weeks into my illness, my younger sister, Carolyn, came to visit and remained to nurse me back to health.

It wasn't until she got there that I was able to hold down soup with vegetables and noodles. I think now that without her I might never have recovered. Did she suspect what was going on? Unconsciously, perhaps?

My own brain was too busy mulling over ideas as I plowed through the novels of Sartre and de Beauvoir between bouts of vomiting and diarrhea. Even recently, when I reread *No Exit* and *She Came to Stay*, my body remembered, and a sickening queasiness came over me.

A month after I recovered, I moved back to the desert with the kids. Daryl remained in the city, hospitalized with his psychosis. His psychologist had insisted on the hospitalization – and the laws in those days were there to support him. I wonder now what else that doctor might have known about what Daryl was doing that made him insist Daryl to go into the hospital. Did Daryl have plans for me similar to his plans for our former neighbor, Sharon?

I spent most of the paycheck he left us on a low-rent house back in Yucca Valley, a wonderful stone house a few miles out of the town itself. The fact that it was made of stones gathered from around the area made the place feel especially safe and secure at a time when not much else in my life felt that way. Back home in the desert again, this time without Daryl, I fell deep into Tolstoy and anything of C. J. Jung's I could get my hands on. Jung's work had an effect on my thinking as powerful as had de Beauvoir's, although not as immediate. I loved also the exotic world Tolstoy opened up to me, remember hoping *War and Peace* would never end, even as I watched the conclusion of that great tome creep nearer. I read at night, since I couldn't sleep for coughing up green phlegm from a bout with bronchitis that I couldn't kick without antibiotics. It was a comfort to lose myself in that exotic world of deep snow and mittens, rather than lost in the world where I and all five children had bronchitis and not enough to eat. When I finally managed to get some money to take them to a doctor, he insisted I take antibiotics as well.

By summer, I'd begun writing poetry and stories on an old typewriter I found at a thrift shop. I hadn't been exposed to much poetry, so I wrote on the order of: "Star light, star bright/All the stars I see tonight/Although I'm sad, my world is Woe/But to you, I'm just a glow." Yuck. But no matter, the poems were for healing. I remember, also, that the poems and stories and essays I wrote began to take over my life. For a while, I wanted to do nothing else with any 'free time' I could find. Then one day when the children came in from play and interrupted me, I had an urge to take that typewriter and bash it over their heads to make them stop bothering me. The next day, I took the machine back to the thrift store. I told myself "someday, but not now."

This was the first time I had a short respite from Daryl's craziness, had only to deal with my own. And the five kids. His hospitalization brought me another gift, too – his disability checks.

Water from a good well was included in the $60 rent, so I planted a garden among countless pottery shards. The place had once been the home of local Indians and the kids spent time searching for old pots hidden in the rocks. Timmy even found a whole olla, which we placed in the local museum. I invited Renee's Brownie troop up to see the pottery shards and other artifacts, then became good friends with the troop leader, Diana. I began baking bread again and making cinnamon rolls. I had to work only two nights a week, using a teenage babysitter who lived in a nearby cabin, to make ends meet. The rest of the time I spent reading. All in all, it was a wonderful few months. For the first time since our marriage eight years before, I felt free and happy and fully alive. Maybe for the first time ever.

Chapter Six
Back to 1972
Close Encounters of the Primal Kind

Seven years after I shot that wounded dog in 1965, during that day in 1972 when dramatically I shed my clothes and fled naked from Daryl, I was feeling free and happy and fully alive, too. In fact, I'd come to feel that way much of the time since I'd started college. My life with Daryl was still a mess, but my real life was elsewhere – at the university. I suppose a great part of my life had been elsewhere for a long time – in that book-enriched world of ideas in my head as I searched for life's meaning. But now the intellectual life that sustained me had become an integral part of my daily life. I loved my two-day-a-week life as a student. I'd arranged to have all my classes on Tuesday and Thursday. That way I only made the ninety-mile-each-way drive to UC Riverside twice a week. My good friend, Diana lived across from the school my children attended and her three children were best friends with mine. A full-fledged earthmother, she actually enjoyed having the kids come over and play until Daryl came home from work. All I had to do was drop them off at school on Tuesdays and Thursday and leave town.

My studies were pure joy. I loved raising questions in class, loved arguing and exploring ideas in and out of class. The only things I missed that day when I traipsed naked, free and fully alive into the cactus-covered mountains were my books, filled with the words of Henry Vaughan and George Herbert, the Metaphysical poets I had planned to reread. And so I found a patch of wash sand and dropped my sweaty body onto it, settled into the soft granite sand, while high cirrus clouds drifted through the pale blue sky over head and let lines like "I saw the universe the other night/Like a great ring of pure and endless light" float through my head and levitate my spirit far beyond what I could see above me.

One of my greatest discoveries at the university had been poetry, something that until then I had neglected reading completely. After that discovery, I enriched my left-brain idea-quest for truth with the metaphorical insights I felt more at home with. They were closer to floating celery.

I wasn't quite sure what to make of one rather literal metaphor that appeared overhead that day embodied in the cirrus clouds that day, though. It was the unmistakable likeness of Jesus, long haired and robed, with arms outstretched. What was that about, I wondered? What was the Universe (or my unconscious) trying to tell me? I lay naked on the bare earth – something about my puny role in a the vastness Mother Earth, Father/Jesus Sky? The corn ball message seemed to have a disturbing erotic flavor as well.

When the sear of sun on my breasts and the pebbles poking into my bare back like the questions poking into my heady bliss became too much, I got up and started toward some rocks in a shady spot beneath a nearby Joshua tree, still somewhat lost in contemplation of the metaphor overhead and its connection to the feminine symbol buried in Vaughn's ring of light. That was the moment when the terrifying buzzzzz of a rattler sawed through the last remnants of my ecstasy and sent me flying a foot into the air and two feet to the side, armpits and gut all jangled with terror. I looked back to find the source coiled in the shade of the rock I was about to sit on. There's nothing like a confrontation with death to harsh a mellow. And rattlers had always been a major nemesis for me and for the magical worlds I'd created to live in. Despite all I had done to conquer my fear of this monstrous metaphor and actual primal danger, a part of me still remained as terrified as I'd been during my first two encounters.

~

The aforementioned first encounter happened as my dad and mom were driving up the rut road to our camp in the canyon with me in the back seat. Suddenly my Mother started yelling, "Rattler! Rattler! Stop the car, Ernest!"

My dad jammed on the brake, then both of them hurried out of the car and headed behind it, leaving me trapped and confused inside. I'm not sure how old I was, but I must have been around three or so because I couldn't even see out the back window of the car to find out where they went or what they were doing or what was making such a horrid noise. I remember how I kept jumping up higher and higher on the back seat, trying to get a glimpse of them from the window, but all I could see was the top half of the mountain behind us. I could barely hear their alarmed shouts because my head was dominated by that loud, brain- numbing buzz. The air was thick with it. Then there was a big bang and the horrid buzzing stopped.

I could tell from the diminishing sound of their voices that my parents were now moving away from the car. They must have been burying the snake, but all I knew was that something really terrible was happening out there and that now they were abandoning me. Inside the car was getting hotter and hotter by the minute. Time seemed to stop altogether but my fear did not. All I can remember was intense heat and a terror that went on and on and on.

When the car door finally opened, both my parents seemed surprised to find me crying and afraid and curled up into a ball. They kept telling me over and over about how rattlers could kill me and how they had killed the rattler instead and that I was now safe. I still had no idea what the this terrible rattler that could kill me was, but I knew in my bones that this was a danger unlike anything else I knew The unafraid little girl who chased wharf rats down storm drains and ran barefoot on the wild canyon's sand to explore its wonders had encountered a whole other dimension to her world, one that stopped her in her joyful tracks.

My second rattler encounter was even more traumatic – and truly dangerous. We, five year-old me, both parents, and my little sister who must have been a toddler, were for the first time actually living year round on the homestead. Our home base while they were building a cabin was the Indian Campground/Can-Tree Springs area, where cattlemen had camped before my mother had homesteaded the place. A large army tent housed our cots, although it was full-on summer and we often dragged the cots outside for sleeping; our table sat outside, too, under one of four large piñons. A wooden and burlap cooler hung from a second piñon, and our stove was the campfire a few feet away.

At the time of that second encounter, my Aunt Evelyn (my father's sister), Uncle Vernie and two boy cousins, Jimmy and Jerry, were up for a weekend visit. The cousins were three and four years older than I was and eager to be free of the pesky little girl cousin that the adults kept making them take with them when they went to play in the wild canyon they had come to visit. And, truth be told, I was not eager to go with them either; they seemed more excited about killing lizards and horned toads and squashing every bug or ant they could find than anything I recognized as play.

My cousins and I headed for the little mountain across from our camp that my mother called Rocky Mountain. Rocky Mountain might have been smaller than the other mountains that lined our canyon, but it was steeper and more difficult to climb since it was little more than a collection of interesting rock formations that jutted out of the scrub oak, piñons and Spanish dagger cacti that had managed to find enough rooting to grow from the decomposing granite surrounding the formations. I loved each and every formation: the twenty-foot high stack of "pancake" rocks, the "three bears" rocks, "Santa Claus" rock – and the more accessible "shelf rocks" nearer the mountain's bottom that we could actually climb onto. The "shelf" was where my cousins and I climbed that morning, and we were standing on the bottom shelf when suddenly that same horrid buzzing as before suddenly dominated the air around us.

Sometime during that initial, paralyzing moment of fear, my cousins had fled, and when I returned to survival mode, I found myself trapped and alone on a rock shelf at the bottom of Rocky Mountain, held tight by unbearable buzz of a rattler chain-sawing though my head. I knew well I had to get out of there but didn't know which way to run. The sound seemed to come from all directions, and the shelf was thickly lined with scrub oak on both sides where the monster could be hiding. I had no idea which way was the safe way, the way my cousins went to get out. Desperate in my terror, the air and world around me seemed to have an eerie green tint. All the while, I kept hearing over and over what my mother had been saying ever since we moved to the canyon, "Watch out for rattlers; they can kill you," as if that very sound were branding those words into my skull.

And now the killer snake was coming to get me. To kill me. I looked down at the sandy wash below the shelves, which looked to be about as far down as our old house was high. A pile of sharp rocks sat just in front of the sand. But the snake was much worse than any rocks.

I flung myself as far out from the rock shelf as I could, and somehow my feet reached the soft sand of the wash. I tore off toward our tent, kept going right past Mother, who was sprinting over with her .22 Marlin, my dad, Uncle Vernie and my two cousins right behind her. When I reached our tent, I leapt onto the bed and huddled there, afraid the rattler would kill my family and cousins and then come for me.

After what felt like forever, everyone came back to camp. Yet I wasn't at all sure this was my real family. Nothing around me felt real at all. Mother tried to tell me she had killed the snake and cut its head off. "It's not dangerous anymore," she kept saying.

She took my hand, tried to pull me off the bed to take me back to bottom of Rocky Mountain with her and show me the dead snake.

"No!" I grabbed back my hand, firmly cemented in my terror. "It will kill us!" That's when Daddy picked me up and locked my frantically struggling body in his arms and carried me to the kill spot. "See, Susie," he kept saying when we got there, "We cut his head off. It's all ok now."

Still fighting to free myself, I refused to look down, as if the mere sight of that snake would kill me. Then Uncle Vernie brought the shovel, held it up to my face, and my eyes couldn't escape the horrible snake head, with its gaping mouth and terrible fangs. I wrenched myself out of my daddy's arms and ran back to the bed in the tent where I felt at least a little bit safe.

This encounter finished off the brave little wharf rat hunter, and although she worked hard to fight her way back, her days of living in a benign world full of wonders was gone forever.

For weeks afterward I remained paralyzed with fear, knowing that certain death lurked out there in the brush, waiting to wend its sharp and poisoning fangs. I could feel rattlers behind every scrub oak, juniper and sage. I wouldn't go near Rocky Mountain for a long, long while. It took several days before I could make myself walk outside the tent by myself rather than have someone carry me to the outhouse. Even then I would hop from rock to rock to get to the privy or sit out by the campfire. I felt safer up off the ground, but every rustle of wind in the brush sent a rush of blood to my head and flood of terror deep into my bowel.

As the summer went on, the fear began to fade somewhat, and I slowly allowed myself to walk on bare ground again as long as I threw small rocks into each bush before walking by it. I also found another safe place in the playhouse my Uncle Kit moved to the canyon for me and found great comfort in catching various bugs, lizards and horned toads to bring in and save from rattlers. Yet even as I hid out in my little refuge, I shivered over all the rattlers that could be hiding in bushes around the playhouse. I felt as tiny and vulnerable as the little ladybugs crawling up my window screen in the face of all the danger I now knew was out there in the wild world. The magical wonders I loved were out there too but seemed as fragile as I had learned I was.

Chapter Seven
How to Dispatch a Rattler

Over the next years, I worked hard to conquer my fear. Gradually, I began to walk on the ground without throwing rocks into each and every bush, to enjoy the feel of my bare feet on sand again and to run up mountains without fearing for my life. By the time I was eight or nine I had forced myself to catch non poisonous garter and gopher snakes and allowed them to wind their scaly bodies around my arms, crawl up around my shoulders and down my other arm – leaving their pungent snaky smell on my skin. A little creepy, but interesting, too. When a garter snake I was playing with bit my index finger and only caused two little stinging holes where bubbles of blood seeped up, fangs no longer seemed quite so scary.

Eventually encountering rattlers around the cabin, in the road, garden and in the shade of rocks and brush everywhere became common place, usually one or two a week. As was the custom, Mother would grab her .22 and shoot them. But the first rattler I encountered on all my own was soon after we moved into our newly built cabin when I ran down the mountain and into our strawberry patch. I flew over the black diamond as it coiled in a shady spot between two leafy strawberry plants.

This rattler didn't make a sound, but I did. I yelled RATTLER and Mother was right there with the .22. I didn't flinch but stood off to one side and watched as she shot its head off. We buried the head for safety, but rather than burying the rest of the snake too, mother showed me how to skin the snake and pin its skin to a board to dry in the sun. It would be my hatband, she told me, as we carried the naked, stinking carcass across the wash and flung it out for the coyotes to find.

I was too young to use the .22 yet, but I soon learned to slay these dragons my own way, with rocks and sticks. Not when quick-draw Mother was around with her rifle of course, but whenever I came across one while I climbing around the mountains or playing in the wash up canyon. Then it was up to me alone to dispatch the harbingers of death. I still felt the same terror but was determined not to let that hinder me. Rattlers, like that terror, I had learned, were a part of life that had to be dealt with. And they could be killed just as I could. And I could be their killer.

I discovered how to get a snake to break its coil by throwing large rocks at it. Then I would go after it with a long stick with as much of a fork at the end as I could find and pin it behind the head. I used another long stick to push its neck in and grind and grind until the rattler was disabled, then would mash the head under a good-sized rock and grind some more until the head separated from the body, or was attached only by ragged skin.

I became almost as efficient at this method as Mother was with her rifle, and gradually made a point of using shorter and shorter sticks. Although that gave me better leverage to get the head off, the main reason I did it was I think the same bravado that led me to kill them in the first place. And the more proficient I got at it, the quicker the fearful bloodrush a rattler sent into my head and belly transformed into a powerful sense of invincibility. I gave everyone I knew a dried skin hatband, whether they wanted it or not. The signs of my invincibility became a badge worn everywhere.

I suppose all that was why years later when I stood naked in the mountains that day, I automatically sprang into action, located a broken scrub oak branch about eight inches long, a few rocks, and went after the rattler. When the poor snake tried to crawl away, I went into my usual routine, ran up behind and attacked it with the broken oak branch, jamming its neck against the ground. Except this time I wasn't feeling powerful. Instead, I became keenly aware of my thudding heart, tingling armpits, of the smell of sweat from my own body mixed with that of the snake. Aware, too, of my clenched jaw – and of the short stick in my other hand. Did I really need to be doing this, especially barefoot and naked? And why did I attack this squirming and frightened snake that had only tried to warn me in the first place? Hadn't I proved I could dispatch such dangers long ago?

I removed the oak branch from the poor rattler's neck, stepped back and watched as the rattler slithered toward safety. Pulling in a deep breath, I settled down on one of the rocks in the Joshua Tree's shade and let my kaliedoscoping thoughts and feelings settle too.

I remembered something, then, something that seemed to have nothing to do with rattlesnakes: The Hurricane Chaser roller coaster.

I was sixteen, seven months pregnant and making a point of going to see the woman Daryl told just me he had slept with. We had only been married seven months. Daryl had confessed his "crime" when he came home after being out all night. He was supposed to have been "out with the boys," a lie from the start, apparently, since he said he'd intended to connect with his old flame all along.

I'd spent seemingly endless and painful hours that night pacing and wide awake, wondering what had happened to Daryl – and being even more bewildered about what had happened to the me I once knew. The huge bulge of my pregnant belly had alienated me from the physical self I'd always known. Flooded with the melodrama of hormones, I no longer recognized even the remnants of my former strong and adventurous self in the pitiful, frightened creature helplessly pacing the floor. We had no phone, no radio or television to give me any connection to the outside world.

Daryl's confession the next morning when he returned did more than reach in and rip through the rest of me, leaving me feeling like a naked rabbit carcass hanging from a rope; it stripped away any remnant of who I had been when I fantasized he and I becoming like the loving Joad family. And killing that delusion must have somehow released my lost former self, the rattlesnake killer. I sprang into action, demanding that Daryl take me to see my rival. He certainly didn't want to do that but was unable to say no to this side of me that he had never encountered, and soon I found myself at her door ringing the bell.

When a young woman opened the door, I asked if she was Jody. She said yes and I held out the key to the little apartment Daryl and I rented in El Monte. "Here you go, then," I said. "You can have him."

I remember her look of total puzzlement as if she had no idea who in the world I was. "Daryl," I said. "I'm his wife."

"I... I...I," she stuttered, pulling back her hand. "I...I don't even know if I want him."

"Well, if you do, he's yours," I dropped the key onto her porch. "I certainly don't care." With that, I turned and walked away.

I moved back to my parent's house, where I was still living two months after Renee was born when Jody came to see me there. She said she was sorry that she'd gotten involved with him and that he was all mine (This I had guessed since he had been trying to get me to move back with him ever since I left). She wondered if we could go out together, have some fun, maybe. She said she'd like to get to know me. "How about the Fun Park at Huntington Beach? There's a great roller coaster there."

Although I had never ever seen a roller coaster and hadn't been so much as to the store without the baby, I decided to fully confront this threat before me and go out with her. My sister Carolyn happened to be home and said she'd watch little Renee.

The Hurricane Chaser was visible long before we actually reached the Fun Park, its massive wooden frame towering above the beach area like a mountain range dominating the landscape. As we got out of Jody's little Ford, I could hear the screams of riders and the clatter of wheels on the track as the cars raced up and down the steep hills.

After going on a few of the tamer rides, Jody asked if I was ready for the "coaster." Of course I was ready, I told her, and soon we were racing up and down the steep hills laughing and screaming with delight. On time second we rode, and at a particularly steep downward descent, Jody dared to stand. I snapped into action and stood also, remained standing when she sat back down. In fact I stood on each and every descent the rest of the ride. And the next ride. At first Jody tried to match my bravado but soon gave up. It was clear which one of us was the rattlesnake killer, and that same surge of triumphant invincibility as when I dispatched a rattler rushed through my entire being.

But Jody was not the rattler who was threatening my sense of self, I realized as I sat there under the Joshua tree. The real rattler was still around, still inhabiting the life I led. At least for now; I had been building my escape route for some time.

I fully understood, too, in that naked moment, that Daryl was the snake whose head I wanted to grind off with a sharp stick. In case you're wondering just who *was* this snake I'd married and how in hell did I hook up and stay fifteen years with someone as unreliable as he was. Someone who lied more often than told the truth, who couldn't be trusted to go to the store for milk without at times disappearing for hours, sometimes days. Someone whose weeks of job searching I once learned had meant spending endless days at the beach, accompanied, I assumed, by the women who belonged to all the bras and panties and blankets I found among the beer bottles when I opened the car trunk one day. So if you are wondering how I remained living such a crazy and out-of-control life for so long, well, so am I. I'm still not sure – other than being at first a teenager and then a young woman, confused and with little resources to care for her five children, each of whom arrived almost yearly, thanks to the era's wholly inefficient birth control devices, children who loved Daryl and had no idea of how incredibly irresponsible and unreliable their father actually was. But what I do know is that to some extent our getting together in the first place was a result of finally being seduced by a movie.

Chapter Eight
1954
I Follow Hollywood

By the time I was in the seventh grade, I had managed to adjust to our move from the canyon back to Bassett. I had plenty of friends, went to parties, where we danced and played spin-the-bottle. Although we still spent most of each summer back in the canyon, I'd learned to enjoy a few city things, especially the Tarzan movies at the Tumbleweed Theater. Movies were much more fun to watch after they were finished than while they were being made. Tarzan had given me hours afterward of swinging from imaginary trees as I sounded the Tarzan call and saved people in trouble. I liked television, too, and could even recognized some of the episodes I'd seen being made in Frontiertown. And the ocean thirty miles away was wonderful. But just when I fully settled in and felt comfortable with this city life, Mother left my father and moved us back to the canyon.

At first, none of us kids, myself, Carolyn, now age nine, nor my brother Danny, age five, knew that Mother actually planned to divorce my father. We just thought we were up in the canyon for the summer as usual. We *had* seen increased violence between them – not from our dad, who'd had to lock himself in the bathroom a couple times while Mother tried to chop down the door with a butcher knife. Another time I remember her trying to kick him in the stomach right after he returned from the hospital from an appendix removal.

Once he actually had to break down that bathroom door when Mother locked herself inside with poison (or so she said) and the same butcher knife. And he was always having to go out and drag her out of bars after he came home from work. I wonder now if more had happened between them than I understood, if my rock-solid father had not been as rock-solid a husband as he appeared to be around the house. I'll never know, of course. At the time it just seemed like Mother was even crazier than normal during this period, and extremely mean.

At any rate, I started the eighth grade back in Yucca Valley, the small town twelve miles on a dirt road from our cabin. The one-room school I'd attended in Frontiertown, a mere eight miles down the dirt road from our cabin, no longer existed, and it had only gone to the sixth grade in the first place. Yucca Valley, on the other hand, had a growing population of around a thousand. Perhaps two thousand. I didn't measure such things by numbers at the time. At any rate, Mother moved us from the canyon to the little town itself soon after school began.

At the school in Yucca Valley, I found myself regarded as a "new" girl, again, and a "city girl" to boot. None of classmates in Yucca Valley knew anything about the earlier school house that had once existed in Frontiertown four miles north of town, probably because most of their families were fairly new in the area. The fact that I'd lived and spent every summer of my life on a homestead in the wild mountains behind town wasn't even believable to them. The girls decided to hate me – mainly because I had grown some sizable boobs and knew how to dance, and because every boy in the eighth grade and even a few in high school decided that the city girl was exciting and that they "liked" me. I have to admit I enjoyed this heady surge of male attention and the constant stream of "steadies" it brought.

This attention, however, led to a number of painful events, such as the time the girls pulled off my sweater in the bathroom, then went out and told the boys I wore falsies. When I became outraged over their lie, they said sarcastically, "Why don't you take your sweater off and show them, then, Susie." The girls devised many other plans to humiliate me, but everything they did served to give my sexuality more power and make the boys "stick up for me." I simply held in my belly, raised my chest as I walked, and bowled all the boys over. It was almost as empowering as killing rattlers.

If I'd had a choice, though, I would have chosen to be accepted by those girls, which is why I continued trying to let everyone know that I wasn't just some stupid city girl. I sometimes hunted and shot cottontail rabbits to show my homesteader's skills, hanging them on a clothesline in the back yard to skin and gut for all to see like little flags announcing who I really was before frying them up our dinner. This probably didn't work wholly in my favor. None of the girls and very few of the boys had ever hunted game. Around this time, I also skinned a bobcat that had been hit on the highway, salted and nailed its hide to a piece of plyboard to dry in our yard. It stank to high heaven. My schoolmates, male and female paraded by to witness this. None of them commented.

Even with my social and family life in shambles, I managed to graduate from the eighth grade as valedictorian. School work was the one thing I could control, and it was something I did better than anything else. However, I didn't think of schoolwork in terms of earning academic honors (had in fact never heard of a valedictorian before becoming one) but because I loved learning – like most children before our school systems drain that out of them. For me, learning about life and the world around me brought a kind of joy that sustained me. As I child, I had wanted to learn as much as I could about the plants, animals and rocks around me and the stars overhead. I can remember my father telling me about how far away in time and space the countless stars were, and how many years it took for their light to even reach us. I must have been about five years old. Concepts like this early on gave me a perspective on how transitory human life and dramas – including the dramas in my own life and family – really were in the ultimate scheme of the universe. That has always been a great comfort.

Most after-school time while I was in the eighth grade, was spent babysitting Danny and Carolyn while Mother was out around town. During the day she worked as a salesperson in a real estate office. At night she frequented bars, especially the Silver Dollar and had made friends with a woman named Sonja, who owned the place. My mother was comfortable in bars, perhaps because she had spent much of her childhood hanging around her father's bar in Juarez. She was never a heavy drinker, would get buzzed after two or three beers. Her comfort from bars was not so hot for her children, unfortunately. Meanness would come with her buzz. And for a while she was going out with a some man I occasionally saw sleeping in the ditch in front of the Silver Dollar bar. His clothes were always rumpled and he stank to high heaven with booze – and he looked so much like a sodden version of my father that it gave me the creeps.

Meanwhile, Danny, now age five, developed a flare for starting fires in vacant lots around town – of which there were many. Around this time, he, along with the five-year-old son of the bar owner, "robbed" the cash register of the Silver Dollar. Back in 1952, cash registers often went unwatched in the small desert town, where everyone knew everyone else. So it was an easy heist for the two little boys. They put the money in a paper sack, along with the gun they found in the cash drawer (well, I guess people weren't *too* trusting then), and hid the sack somewhere on the mountain. Danny confirmed my suspicions about it years later, confessing that he could never find their 'stash' again.

Mother had also developed the habit of bringing home Marines (who were stationed the base twenty miles away) after the bars closed at 2:00 a.m. This went on all through my eighth grade year. She would wrench me out of sleep at night and insist that I entertain the younger Marines in the living room, while she talked to older sergeant-types in the kitchen. I doubt anything ever went farther on her part than a bit of drunken flirting, so I don't think she expected anything sexual to occur in the entertaining she required of me either. And it didn't. But these events certainly interfered with my rest on school nights. I spent many late nights/early mornings sitting on the sofa bored and half-asleep, while half-drunk young Marines from seventeen to twenty-five told me their life stories. Not one of them ever tried to do more than that.

One night, however, was different. It was the night before my graduation and when Mother came into the bedroom and woke me, I refused to get up. I told her "NO!" that I was valedictorian and had to be at school by 6:00 a.m. to start decorating and practicing for the graduation ceremony to be held at noon. She demanded several times that I get up, but I held my ground. "I'll get you later, you little slut," she finally hissed, her beer breath almost enough to ignite the air. It took some time before my heart quit pounding and I could slip off to sleep.

Sometime later, I was awakened by her pulling me out of bed by the hair. "I'll teach you to disobey me," she said, and carried on with more 'little slut' type endearments. She dragged me into her bedroom, still by the hair, all the while shaking my head from side to side. With one hand, she began rifling through her top dresser drawer for the black leather belt she kept there for just such occasions. When she whipped out the belt, she let go and came at me swinging the strap.

I have no idea why I did what I did, anymore than I understand why I had finally refused to go along with her plans for me in the first place, or why I didn't just duck and take my punishment. But enough was enough, I guess. I took a step forward and punched her squarely on the nose. She fell to the floor, either knocked out or passed out, I'll never know for sure which. I felt sorry for her lying there, so I took a pillow from her bed and put it under her head, then covered her with a blanket and went back to my own bed. It was like seeing the wicked witch of the west melt right there in front of me.

Did this act give me the same rush of power as killing rattlers, collecting steadies, and knocking out school tests in record time? I don't remember. I suspect that by now I had incorporated that power to the degree that using it was no longer any great event. I just did these kinds of things: vanquish dangers, was invincible, and that was that.

My inner confidence, aka bravada, had grown to such an extent that at times I put myself in real danger, and not just with rattlers. And this was long before Daryl came into the picture. Like the time I ran away at age 13, the summer after the eighth grade – simply hitchhiked off into the sunset to start a new life with my best friend, Gloria, who had two alcoholic parents who drank steadily, rather than one who got crazy wild and had nightly escapades.

1952 was a conservative era long before hippie-hitching, yet hitchhike our way toward LA was what we did. I had $13.64 saved up from my job selling hot dogs at a local dude ranch that summer, and an ice pick in my little purse. I was determined to make it all the way to San Francisco to start my new life. It was fourteen years too early for the Summer of Love, and Gloria and I hadn't a cell of peace-love-dope in our bodies. I was confident we'd do fine in our new life. After all, I was a working girl and experienced at selling hot dogs for a whole $1.00 an hour, while watching my brother and sister at the same time. There were bound to be lots and lots of hot dog stands in San Francisco.

Mother was off to LA herself that night to see my father for some reason, unfortunately. It couldn't have been a liaison, since she took her bar owner friend, Sonja, with her and promised that she'd be back by morning. I decided to go anyway, so after Danny and Carolyn were safely asleep, I stuck pillows under my covers, climbed out the window and met up with Gloria. I don't remember if we took any clothes with us, though we must have brought small satchels with us. At any rate, we walked to the highway and stuck our thumbs out for adventure.

We were soon picked up by two Marines. Lo and behold they were going to L.A. for the weekend, which most Marines did. Gloria got in the front and I got in the backseat. One of the Marines got in back with me. I'd had enough experience with Marines to not be afraid of them. Actually, there wasn't much I *was* afraid of – and if there were, I wouldn't admit it, even to myself. Especially to myself.

So off we went. Both Marines downed beer as we drove, a driving practice quite common in those days. My Marine began sliding his arm around me, getting more and more octopussy, no matter how many times I removed the arm. It was taking more and more effort to remove it, and when I did, his hand would snake back around and land on my breast. He was quite strong. Somehow, the ice pick I'd brought along didn't seem like a viable option for stopping him. So about forty or fifty miles from LA, during a long stretch of farmland that was hidden from the highway by a line of eucalyptus trees, I asked the driver to pull over so I could "use the bushes." Actually, I had waited until we got near the pig farms – I knew that section of road fairly well from all my family's weekend trips back to the canyon – and when Marines stopped, Gloria and I jumped out. She followed me as I ran through the darkness toward the stinky pig pens across the field behind the trees.

The Marines got out, too, and started to follow, calling out our names, but the stench soon discouraged them and they went back to the car and, eventually, drove off. We cowered behind a hedge between the pens and a darkened farm building, nearly throwing up from the odors that had saved us. When I think back now, I wonder if the Marines would have thrown us out of the car sooner without us having to use that ruse if we had admitted we were thirteen and not seventeen.

When we were relatively sure the Marines weren't coming back, we made our way to the highway and started walking toward LA, keeping to the eucalyptus trees that lined the fence along this thirty mile stretch of then empty highway between Colton and Pomona. There wasn't much traffic at that time of night, mostly semi-trucks, so we didn't have to keep hidden most of the time. I don't know how long we walked, but it seemed like forever. We weren't getting very far. And it was way past our bedtimes. One other thing: I swear I saw Mother and Sonja pass by us in our station wagon on the other side of the divided highway, as they headed back home.

I don't know how or even if it was decided upon, but I know that after a while I not only failed to hide but stuck out my thumb when one of those semis came by. After all, trucks traveled long distances – and truck drivers had to be safer than the Marines. The semi driver who stopped was a large middle-aged man with a belly that could hardly fit behind the steering wheel. He appeared very fatherly. And sure, he'd take us at least as far as his apartment in L.A., he said, and who knew, he might just drive us up to San Francisco as well. I climbed in beside him and let Gloria sit by the door.

We both fell asleep right away, but we hadn't gone far before I woke up and found his arm around me doing a little exploration of my breast. I edged away and started a conversation with him, but that didn't stop his hand's attempt at geographical exploration.

I had another idea; we had a girlfriend, I suddenly told him, a few miles away in Bassett. She planned to go with us and was expecting us to come by and get her. And I was sure she would love to spend the night at his apartment too. Of course, there was no such girl waiting for us, but I knew Bassett well, and I had a plan for escape. He seemed more than intrigued, so I told him she lived about a mile ahead, on Orange Blossom Avenue. It was only a block out of his way. Practically drooling, he said he was more than happy to pick her up as well.

I actually did know a girl who lived on Orange Blossom Avenue. Her name was Dorothy Coffman. She had been my best friend back when I lived in Bassett. I still wrote to her, and about a year after that night I ran away, she would introduce me to Daryl. However, I had no intention of picking Dottie up that night.

Once the driver stopped the truck in front of Dottie's house, Gloria and I got out to "knock on her window to wake her up." Instead, we went straight through her back yard and took off over her back fence, then ran a long way down a dirt alley and hid in a huge weeping willow that took up the entire front yard of an abandoned and dilapidated house. When I'd lived in Bassett, I had believed the house was haunted and had made a point of going out of my way to avoid the place. Now, like the stinky pig farm, I was grateful for it being there.

I figured the truck driver wouldn't hang around long when we didn't reappear, and if he did happen go to Dottie's door, her huge muscular father would handle him just fine. After some time had gone by, Gloria and I began making our way through the back streets toward El Monte, finally getting back on the highway an hour or so later when we reached the dry riverbed by the gypsy camp. As we stumbled across the bridge leading into El Monte, dawn was lighting up the eastern horizon.

We were about half-way across the bridge when a sleek black car drove by. It stopped and backed up toward us. A gorgeous guy in the passenger seat leaned his blond head out the window. "Where are you headed?" he asked.

"San Francisco," I said. "But we're going through L.A. first."

"Hop in, then," the driver said. "We can take you as far as L.A." I could see he was good looking, too, with dark hair. He looked to be around twenty-five like his companion. Clearly, they thought they'd hit the jackpot.

I considered the offer, but only for a few seconds. Here we were, a hundred miles plus from home, and since it was now morning, I figured we'd burned our bridges. We had but a few dollars with us to get started in our new life, and we'd already had two narrow escapes in the few hours we'd been on the road. Hmmm. What should we do?

"Okay," I said. The blond was already out, pushing his seat

out of the way so we could slide in to the back seat. And that's what we did.

Only this time, we were lucky. Very lucky. We hadn't gone far when the driver pulled over and both of them gave us a closer inspection. "Oh my god," the driver said. "How old are you guys anyway?"

"Seventeen," we both answered at once, the way we'd been saying all night.

"No fucking way," the blond guy said. "How old are you, really?

Well, we were too tired to argue and finally confessed to being thirteen and running away. I will always be grateful to those two young men, who decided to save us and drive us the hundred plus miles back to Yucca Valley. They even stopped at a drive-in to feed us. When we tried to order a coke with our hamburgers, they wouldn't let us – said we were too young and could only order milk. They paid for our food too.

Mother's station wagon was parked in the yard when we arrived, so we drove on by. I got out a block away and sneaked back in the window. When I came into the kitchen all rumpled, Mother said something like, "It's about time you got up, you lazy thing." But she was in a good mood and didn't even suspect anything – mainly since my sister Carolyn had covered for me. Mother had sent her in to get me up, but when Carolyn discovered the pillows under the covers, she went back out and told mother I wasn't feeling well and would get up soon. Loyalty should be my sister Carolyn's middle name.

I'm not sure anyone at school ever believed Gloria's and my story, either. After while, we began to wonder about it ourselves. That night seemed like some kind of weird dream.

I was only a couple months into my freshman year at 29 Palms High School when Mother announced she was "going back to your father" and said we would move back to Bassett. I was happy about the reunion but not about leaving Yucca Valley after living a year and a half there. I had finally become accepted – not enough to get into the cheerleading squad – but I was going steady with a senior who was a star quarterback of 29 Palms High School football team. Uprooted and back in Bassett again, I looked up my friend Dottie and started El Monte High in mid-semester. At least a few of my other old friends from elementary school were there, too, so I didn't feel completely alone. It was during that first month back that Dottie and I went to see *Rebel without a Cause,* and I fell head over heels in love with James Dean. As in love as a fourteen-year-old can be, anyway, with a screen idol. Dean was already dead by then, but naturally that only made my love stronger.

I began to adjust again, then in the middle of my second semester at El Monte High, my parents decided we should move twenty miles away to La Puente, where I would attend La Puente High. This would be the third high school of my freshman year. Mother had recently purchased the Great Books and had begun getting messages from Aristotle that she would record in automatic writing every afternoon in her darkened bedroom. Apparently, it was Aristotle who told her to move to La Puente. La Puente High had something like three thousand students, and I knew none of them.

I wandered around campus feeling like an alien. I had never felt like an alien before, even with all the moving back and forth we did. Up until now it had been the other kids that had felt like aliens to me. Yet in this densely populated school, I was completely lost and alone. To get rid of the ache in my chest, I would go home after school and spend hours in our backyard singing, "When You Walk Through a Storm." I'd sing it over and over, while endless freight trains rolled by. I needed the noise cover, since everyone in the family disdained my singing and would pull out the old cliché that I "couldn't carry a tune in a bucket." True enough, but singing that song was one of the few comforts I had in my new city life. That and reading and doing school work. And dreaming of James Dean.

Then James Dean himself walked into my life. Sort of. Oh,

Daryl's hair was darker and he was taller than Dean. But Daryl had the same sulking walk, the pouting lips, the surprise when the cheeks caved in mid way when he smiled. Both Dean and Elvis had that attribute, although I hadn't come across Elvis yet. Daryl was like the two rolled into one. Like Elvis, he had that subtle, mocking lift of one side of his top lip when he smiled.

At age eighteen, Daryl had already been in Juvenile Hall (though someone as cool as he was would never use any term but "juvie") and had a "record" for stealing cars. How romantic and misunderstood was that?! He even had deliciously alcoholic parents and seven sisters who adored him. The week I met him, he had just come back from picking fruit near Fresno. I had recently finished reading *Grapes of Wrath,* and far from feeling sorry for the Joads, I envied them. They were a family who struggled and loved together, and they had a real life in a tough world I recognized. Just like Daryl's family. Starved for family connection, I could turn even Steinbeck's painful masterpiece into a romantic dream he never intended.

And, Daryl had a real feel for the language of emotions, a trait that even today I am somewhat deficient in. He spoke as easily about the way he felt as most guys spoke about cars or sports, neither of which interested Daryl.

When it came to boys and later to men, those I was attracted to always had certain characteristics. They were always out of the mainstream like I was; they were always "Rebels" (with a capital R). Chemistry was probably number two, but facility with language was right up there with it. Like the character in the movie, *A Fish Called Wanda,* who writhes on the floor when a man speaks "foreign" to her, I writhed inside when a man used metaphor or symbolic allusions. And speaking English was plenty good enough for me. Whatever else a male lacked, I could easily make up for with a little romantic gilding. I was an expert at that.

Daryl was a high school dropout, just as I became when I ran off with him a few months later, so we could pick grapes and have a real life. But Daryl had also read books I hadn't yet read, modern books. *Catcher in the Rye* and *Lord of the Flies* are two I remember, although where he'd come across Salinger and Golding I can't imagine. Juvie, I guess. Best of all, he spoke metaphor.

I remember one night in particular when we were "parked" with two other couples on a hill above El Monte. Daryl and I walked to a place where we could sit on rocks and talk as we stared down into the spread of city lights below. I must have said something about how beautiful it looked, because he said, "Yes, it seems beautiful from here, but when you go down into those starry-looking valleys, you find it's no different from where you were in the first place." He expanded the metaphor and interwove it with pieces of his own experience, but he had me at "starry-looking valleys." And there was incredible feeling in his voice as he said it. I was impressed by the way Daryl, like Dean, could articulate his own painful experience in the world. Although I was a master at articulating ideas out of books, I became dumbstruck when it came to speaking of my own emotional experiences in the world.

It must have been in whatever chemistry was between us or in my own propensities, but I was transported by the way he would describe and imply his unhappiness without whining about it directly. I can see now how unhappy I must have been at home, but I had always steadfastly refused to experience my unhappiness – even though I was spending hours singing about walking through storms each day. I was always sure I could make things better. Sometimes just looking at a flower made things better. I was a person who ran down into the promise of each and every starry valley without questioning. Indeed, I now ran as fast as I could down into Daryl's valley. But except for the sex, it didn't turn out to be very starry. In the end, the stars there turned out to be more like the bright spots of burning refuse at the town dump.

Chapter Nine
1959 & 1947
Unsafe Sex

The fact that I had managed to give birth to five children by the time I was twenty-three (and then later had twins in a commune at thirty-three) might lead you to believe that I liked sex. I won't deny it – though a person doesn't have to like sex to get pregnant, especially in those pre-pill days of ineffective devices. In fact, I didn't come for the first time until after my second child. No one had ever told me about that part of sex; I hadn't even heard the word. Once I discovered orgasms, I developed a half-baked theory that there were two kinds of women in the world: those who came and those who didn't – and those who could became empowered by it the way I had. It sure beat the hell out of killing rattlers. The day after my "first coming," I left Daryl, got a job at Bob's Big Boy restaurant, and took him back only under strict conditions after I found that the neighbor who was babysitting for me at $10.00 a night was pushing the kids around.

I just love putting the situation like that, as if I simply shucked him off like a shell I'd grown out of because of my sudden (and totally accidental) empowerment. But the reality is a lot more pathetic. I had left him once before but took him back just after our first child was born. This time I was seventeen, with both a toddler and an infant. We'd been living hand to mouth for some time. Daryl rarely worked, but he spent time and gas money that I borrowed from my dad out "looking for a job," except that I'd discovered time and again that he was out with 'friends' or at the beach again. Sometimes he'd stay away for two or three days. I'd been borrowing money for rent and for food for the babies from my dad too. I remember eating a lot of eggs and being hungry often.

The final straw came the night Daryl told me he wanted an open marriage where he could have other women and even bring them home. It was not quite the sixties yet, and he certainly wasn't a Mormon, so I have no idea where the idea came from. We had just stopped by my parents' house that afternoon to borrow twenty dollars for baby food, milk and gas, and he'd somehow managed to purchase beer with it as well. I was not happy. All the while, I kept thinking of how the roast in the oven at my parents' house had filled the house with yummy smells, of the way their refrigerator was stocked with milk and everything else, the way it had been while I was growing up. Of course, none of that had anything to do with the accident of my first orgasm, but it did have to do with what happened afterward, which was for me to have Daryl drive me and the babies back to my parents' place afterward, where I told him I was staying for good.

I didn't get that job at Bob's Big Boy right away either, now that I think about it. A person had to be eighteen to work there and I some several months to go. So I stayed with my parents and worked at another local restaurant while Carolyn babysat for me although living with my parents and brother and sister was causing a lot of tension, I worked night shifts because the kids slept well at night, struggling to find rides until I'd saved up enough money to buy a beat up '49 Ford.

As soon as I turned eighteen, I applied and got the job at Bob's. The opening happened to be in Pasadena, thirty miles away. About this time Mother and I had a terrible argument and I moved out. My new apartment was fifteen miles closer to the job, and I was lucky enough to find a neighbor who would watch both kids for $10.00 per night shift. But all that didn't last long. After a few weeks, I was put on the day shift, and at the same time learned about my neighbor's mistreatment of the kids. I desperately needed a babysitter.

Meanwhile, Daryl had been coming around, begging me to come back to him. He didn't have a job, either, and was very willing to be a babysitter while I earned our living – and he agreed to no more going anywhere without me and to me having the car with me even when he did get a job. I hated having to monitor his behavior like that. I felt like a cop but at least it gave me some security. Otherwise, he was completely untrustworthy.

As preposterous as it might seem, I don't know if I ever would have found the gumption to leave him in the first place, nor had the strength to later set and enforce those conditions of our reunion, if I hadn't had a orgasm that night months before I left. It was as if physically coming was the start of my own coming into being as a woman. That primal experience helped me to understand the underpinnings of life and culture. But it's a wonder that Mother didn't ruin all that for me clear back when I was six and she "explained" sex to me.

I have vague memories of the sexual fantasies that I had around the time I was five or six as we bumped up the canyon road in our old Army jeep. I knew nothing consciously about the existence or mechanics of sex at the time. Yet I remember having varied versions of an erotic fantasy where a young boy in my class and I were captured and tied up together so that our "pee pees" touched. It was a fun way to stay occupied during the hour it took to navigate that twelve mile rut road home. Then, a few months later, Mother explained the mechanics in a way that should have scarred me forever.

Throughout my first grade year in the one room schoolhouse, she had been telling me to watch out for kidnappers and never to go anywhere with strangers. She told me, too, that these men did terrible things to little girls. This was necessary information, I suppose, since I usually had to walk to Frontiertown after school and hang around for hours waiting for her or Dad to pick me up. I'd never seen any strangers, aside from the movie people, but some of the men and women I knew who hung around the Red Dog Saloon and the Bowling Alley where my Mother drank seemed to me more like people to watch out for.

I tried to get Mother to tell me just what were the terrible things that men did to little girls, but for the longest time she would only promise to tell me someday when I was old enough. Meanwhile, I concocted my own stories and had the horror narrowed down to men stabbing long knives into little girls' kidneys. Freud would have loved it.

Finally, during the summer following my first grade, after many days of stringing me along with promises to impart that terrible knowledge – school was out and we were stuck in the canyon with no car all week because Dad was using it in the city where he had gone to work when Pioneertown was completed – Mother sat me down at the kitchen table and told me how these men stuck "their huge hard penises inside little girls vaginas again and again and hurt them very bad. Very, very bad." Then, with her next breath, she added, "and that's what men and women do together when they fall in love and get married, and then it's beautiful."

I remember going back outside to play, stunned – not so much from the information about what was done to little girls' vaginas, which seemed to make sense, but by the "then it's beautiful" addition she had made. It was like an alarm going off in my head, an alarm that Mother often set off. Basically, it said that something was seriously wrong with her story. Experience told me that the something wrong was Mother herself. It wasn't that I didn't believe her, rather that something in me – some objective observer – was already aware that she shouldn't be sharing information with me in quite that way. Poor Mother, though I never wanted to probe and see what that might signify about her own sexuality.

It had to have been later in the same summer that she had forced me to tell her which parent I loved best. Unfortunately for me, she wasn't the one. It all went down on a weekend afternoon when my dad was with us. Mother and Carolyn and I had spent hours alone in the jeep while my father went into various places in Yucca Valley, hardware stores and other such places, to "do business." That was an unusual occurrence.

Usually, Mother went in everywhere with him while Carolyn and I waited in the jeep, or played next to it. I'm thinking she must have been newly pregnant with my brother Danny at the time and a bit crazy with the third pregnancy she'd had in her thirties. She was thirty-nine when my brother was born. At my birth she had been thirty-two. Having three kids in seven years that late in her life must have helped push her over the edge and into the violent episodes that followed.

Anyway, each time Dad left us alone in the jeep that day, she started in on me. She kept insisting I tell her which one of the two of them I really loved best. It was okay, she said, if it was him I loved best. Little girls often love their daddy best. It was natural, she assured me over and over.

The more she asked, the more those familiar alarms kept going off. I knew better than to tell her the truth. So for several long stops, I denied that I loved either of them better than the other better. Truthfully, I had never considered the matter before she asked the question, but I knew the answer as soon as she asked it. "I love you both the same," was what I told her again and again, whenever Dad left the car and she started in on me again.

But little by little, she wore me down, until I almost believed that the truth wouldn't make a big difference to her. Besides, I knew she would never let up until I told her. Why I didn't just lie and say that it was her I loved best, I don't know. Maybe this was some kind of turning point with the truth in my young life. Most likely it was because I knew that answer would not have satisfied her anymore than "I love you both the same" did. Maybe I even tried it and don't remember. What I do remember, though, was finally admitting that I loved my dad "just a teeny tiny drop more." "Very teeny weenie," I repeated.

Well, to use one of Mother's favorite clichés, all hell broke loose. I remember her slapping me over and over, shaking me by the hair, then shoving me down on the hard metal floor of the Army jeep. And so on. She went on and on about how I was an ungrateful brat and said that she would never again scrub her "fingers to the bone" washing my clothes. She would never cook me another meal, either. And so forth.

I became a sobbing lump of flesh curled up on the back floor of the jeep. Deep wracking sobs shook my body, and I couldn't stop them even when my dad came back and we drove on to the next business – where Mother repeated her tirade. The spasms and muffled sobs continued as we drove the long, slow twelve miles back to our cabin. Mother must have told him she had punished me for something. But I couldn't stop sobbing even when we got home and simply found a corner somewhere where I continued my silent sobs that had become deep convulsions of breath in a chest that would not stop heaving.

It was my father who finally came in and put his arms around me, then wouldn't leave me be until I told him what had really happened. I could barely utter a word without shuttering spasms, but I didn't have to say much before he got the picture. Then he went in and had a talk with Mother. It was the only time I ever remember him protecting me from her, the only time I ever "told on her", and then only because I was traumatized beyond control.

Surprisingly, Mother never came back at me for telling Dad. Whatever he said to her, it worked. I don't know whether he shamed her or threatened her. If he did threaten her, it would not have been with violence, but with something more subtle. I suspect, though, that he made her see what she had done. I don't believe she ever meant to be destructive, but she always refused to reflect on her behavior when she acted out her own demons – which were many. But whatever it was that Dad said to her that day, he had stopped smiling off into the distance for a while and helped untie me from the railroad tracks. Then he went back to his usual blindness. Mother went back to her usual tactics. And I went back to staying as independent from her as I possibly could at the age of six.

Chapter Ten
1969 – 1973
Slaying Daryl's Demons and Some of My Own

For all of Daryl's crazy and irresponsible behavior, when he wasn't crazy, I believe he loved me as much as he was capable of. I believe this despite my suspicions about a more serious attempt he made to truly undo me that finally dawned on me as I wrote this and faced the evidence. Certainly he loved his children. And they loved him back. Daryl definitely wasn't a 'smiling off in the distance' father, like my own had been. It was more like he was right in there among them – as if he were one of them, which was more than worrisome at times. He wasn't much of a role model, then or now, was always making promises he couldn't keep. Today, as adults, the children are wary of him. Although they love him, each has had negative experiences with him, some of them very painful – such as when he ran off with our seventeen year old son's new car when they were supposed to be reconnecting. Those kinds of things taught them anew not to trust him. Only two of them have kept in any kind of contact with him.

He certainly was not the essence of stability in the family, as my dad had been. I don't know how I could have survived Mother without the stability Dad provided. During those years with Daryl, I was the stable one. Me, as I floundered through emotional adolescence! You can see the trouble we were in.

Before I started college, we would do fun things together as a family. At least during his stable episodes. We had some wonderful adventures. We both loved adventure. On a whim, we would pack up and take off to camp somewhere in the desert overnight, or we would herd the kids into the car and go hunt rabbits for dinner, or decide to spend the weekend camping at the beach sixty miles away, driving vehicles that most people wouldn't take out of town. During the summers, we often traveled down into Baja California to camp on beaches there – which were open and fairly free of other gringos in the mid-sixties. We hunted down mountain wildernesses near Santa Fe and in northern California and camped at their peripheries, walked in to play and fish in streams and pick wild strawberries. I can even remember taking the kids to see the La Brea tar pits and to the LA County Art Museum beside the pits. All of this we did traveling in an old Corvair van that sometimes needed a push start and had slick used tires that I cringe to think about now. A tire was only replaced after it shredded or blew out – which sounds scary to me now. However, we rarely drove on freeways – where the speed limit was fifty-five mph anyway – and there were many less cars on the road in those days.

During the winter months, I would buy a couple extra cans of chili beans or stew each week and stash them away, so that when summer came we'd have a stash of food to take with us on our trips – because finding gas money would be hard enough, even at 25 cents a gallon.

My going back to school changed all that. I'm not sure why I call it "going back" since I only had that one year of high school, and had just one day signed up for an evening college class taught at the Yucca Valley High School campus. It was a British literature class, where I expected to talk about the books I'd already read, such as Dickens and Trollop. Hoping, too, to find out about new books to read and talk about. Of course that wasn't exactly what happened in the class. I did learn about new works, but we mainly examined excerpts and shorter works. Yet for the first time, I was exposed to close reading. It was a whole new level of reading, and I enjoyed hunting for symbols and milking images and metaphor for deeper meaning. This decoding brought a whole new dimension to literature, and I reread other works to unlock them.

The literature class whet my appetite, so after taking a couple more classes, I enrolled full-time at College of the Desert, which was 55 miles away. In those days in California it cost only $10.00 to "matriculate" and take a full slate of classes. And having a high school diploma wasn't required for adults over twenty-one. I was twenty-eight. The low cost and ease of entry constituted a wonderful public service that helped pull many people like me out of poverty's clutches and gave them a chance to contribute to the culture. Unfortunately this is no longer to case anywhere and our entire nation is becoming weaker because of it.

That ease of entry, however, did not mean it was going to be easy. That first full-time semester really kicked my butt – not because of the academic work but because of my living situation. I nearly quit the week after Halloween. The worn out Ford I'd picked up for a hundred bucks as a second car was constantly breaking down from driving more than a hundred miles a day. Just affording the gas was a problem – even at 1969 prices, especially since Daryl was threatening to quit work over me going. All the kids except Jimmy were now in school all day, and Jimmy got out of kindergarten at noon-thirty. It was just barely possible to get all my classes done and drive the 55 miles back home on time to get him – if the car didn't give me any trouble. Then Tim broke his arm. And Jimmy had to have emergency surgery to take out his appendix, which had been chewed up by Ascaris worms in his belly, something the doctor thought he must have picked up on one of our adventures in Mexico. I had just studied Ascaris worms in biology class the week before, and it seemed both amazing and scary to me that I would be subject to a real life demonstration of them in my own family, although the tangle of toothy earthworm-like creatures the doctor exorcized from my son were a whole lot more memorable than the pale drawing in the text book.

After Jimmy's close call, I just didn't see how I could continue with school, at least until the kids were older. To top it off, they all came down with the flu and needed me at home; the car needed a battery, and the tires had no tread left at all. Daryl got even for my going to school by missing enough work to keep us really broke. I needed to start buying Christmas presents for the kids, too, which meant going back to work as a waitress.

When I mentioned my decision to quit school to Gary, a new friend I had met in Spanish class, he convinced me to "just stay until the end of the semester. It's only another month," he said. "Then you won't lose what you've put in so far. That way, when you come back later, you can just pick up where you left off." That sounded reasonable, so I hung in for that final month – and by the end of that semester, it would have taken dynamite to get me out of school.

The gas problem got solved after that first semester, too, when my English professor said he would pay me to help him mark papers, design tests and lead discussion groups on the Shakespeare plays and *Moby-Dick* novel we would be studying the following semester. I jumped at the opportunity but said I'd only do it if he allowed me to design study questions, instead of tests, which I didn't believe had any value. I worked enough as a waitress during the break between semesters not only to get a battery, but to have the spark plugs changed out. And the Christmas present problem was solved when Sears gave us a credit card – fools that they were. I charged new used tires for the car on it as well.

During that second semester, Gary suggested I apply for admission to the University of California in Riverside, where he would be transferring. The university was ninety-six miles southwest of the little town I lived in (the community college had been to the southeast), almost double the distance. It seemed insane, but I applied thinking that I would never be accepted anyway, not to a real university. Well, not only was I accepted, but I was given scholarship help for the coming fall. I wouldn't even have to work as a waitress on weekends. Then, for my birthday, my father gave me the VW bug that he and his new wife were going to trade in. (After twenty-five years, my parents had finally divorced, and Dad had married the woman he would be happy with until her death thirty years later.) My friend Gary was accepted at UCR as well. I'll always be grateful for the practical suggestions he kept making. I doubt I would have ended up with a degree without his guiding me through the labyrinth of academic requirements.

It was at the university that I finally found the intellectual stimulation and challenges I'd been seeking. Community college had been disappointing academically but better than nothing. Very few professors at the community college had been passionately involved with their subjects. At the university, most were – and those were the ones I sought out. At the community college, debate had not been welcome. In fact, a psychology instructor had once warned me that I would have to leave his class if I kept questioning his interpretations, which I found extremely limited and biased.

At the university, the best professors loved my questioning. One professor that I was in awe of even thanked me for "correcting" his interpretation of a Robert Herrick poem. I was shocked. I'd thought I was only asking a question that he would be able to enlighten me about. Professors spoke to me as an equal, even though I clearly wasn't, occasionally asking me for my opinion on papers they were writing for publication. The place was a haven for the intellectual curiosity and thinking that had so long been a part of me. I felt I'd finally found a home for that crucial if not core piece of myself.

One of the great joys during this period was discovering the 17th Century Metaphysical Poets – introduced by a professor I was in awe of – and the Romantic poets of the 19th Century I found in other classes. In brilliant lectures, my favorite professor, Milton Miller, would present each poet in the philosophical context of his time. Then he would actually read a few poems in a voice so rich and melodic that it was all I could do to keep from swooning. Hearing the words and ideas of the poets read in that incredible voice transported me to heights I'd never dreamed of. And once I'd heard *him* read some poems that way, I could hear all the other poems read as they were meant to be read. Then, on my own and in silence, I could transport myself to realms of thought and feeling just out of reach of language. These were realms I had sensed as a child, as I slept out under the night sky or stood alone in the wild canyon. I'd had no idea that poems could also be windows into the mysteries there.

I loved the challenge of having to research and write papers, too, especially papers about literature. Sometimes as many as four fifteen-page papers would be assigned over a weekend – which for me meant between Thursday and the following Tuesday. I had a regular routine of falling asleep on top of my books each evening around ten or so, then getting up around two in the morning to resume studying and writing. My complete immersion in my studies couldn't have been much fun for Daryl, but I had ceased to care.

During the winter nights that I sat up studying, I would lean back against the grill of our old oil heater to keep warm in the drafty house we squatted in. I remember that in the spring when I stripped down and put on a scanty top, I found the flower pattern of the oil stove's grill branded onto the skin of my back.

Attending classes was such a joy that the idea of actually graduating didn't occur to me at all until I got a credit printout that I couldn't at all make sense of. But Gary took one look and pointed out that I had almost enough credits for a degree in English and only needed a few more classes to get a B.A. That was the spring semester before I took my naked jaunt into the wilderness. Originally, I had registered as a psychology major, then just wandered around taking the classes I was interested in, which of course were in literature and poetry. The psychology department didn't offer classes on Freud or Jung or anyone else; it was strictly a program that required things like implanting electric probes in monkeys' brains. And getting a degree had never been the point. Now my friend suggested that

I become an English major. English major? There was such a thing? Didn't almost everyone already speak English? What kind of a scam was that?

The following year, during the final semester before my B.A., several of my professors urged me to apply for a graduate fellowship. They even gave me directions to the office where the applications were available. I had not even considered going beyond my B.A. and had barely gotten used to the idea of any degree at all. I'd finally accepted the idea that getting a degree would be useful, I kept telling myself, for getting jobs other than waitressing. But graduate work? Now that was a really new concept. It sounded elitist, and I wasn't sure I wanted to be that. But just in case, I did go by that office and ask for an application.

The woman behind the glass window made no move to hand me the application I'd requested. Instead, she simply regarded me with disdain and said, "These fellowships are very competitive, you know."

"Oh," I said and turned away from the window, embarrassed. I should have realized, I thought, as I made my way out of the building. I still didn't get what being Phi Beta Kappa meant, and my entire life might have been changed by the attitude of one bureaucratic petty tyrant – if my professors hadn't later intervened.

Keeping myself submerged in studies had changed things at home radically. I had little time for taking trips and didn't much want to take them with Daryl anyway. We did make one miserable trip to the wilderness near Santa Fe and a worse one to Northern California. I'd brought poetry books along, having had too many years of Daryl's dramas, too many years of his lies, too many wounds from his behavior. I'd become anaesthetized from the pain that finding out about his affairs once brought, as I was numbed from the humiliation I once felt during times such as when I overheard Daryl and Sharon make fun of the way I used a toothpick. Etcetera. I just didn't care anymore.

At first, during those nights while I was studying and sleeping on my books, Daryl watched television with the kids. But eventually, he started going out – and staying out late nights, without even making up excuses. I never asked him where he was. As long as he was somewhere else, I was happy.

Then, in an instant, on May 1, 1973, everything changed. Especially me.

The night before it happened is mostly a blur of studying for the four mid-terms scheduled for the next day. Daryl had gone out and wasn't back when I finally fell asleep after 2:00 a.m. He came in sometime around 3:00 a.m. and woke me. I remember that he was covered with dirt and that when I asked him about it, he said that he'd been outside writhing and crying in the driveway because I had stopped caring for him.

"Suddenly, I just couldn't stand it," he said. "To never see your face again when you look at a flower." Too little, too late, as they say these days. His words were not to be trusted. I wanted only to go back to sleep to be ready for my midterms, so I wasn't really listening. And maybe without meaning to, Daryl was telling me something else entirely, something, as I said earlier, I hadn't ever thought of until I started writing about my own life. It was a lot like what would happen to me when writing a novel and I would suddenly realize what the narrative had set up for what was to happen to my character – except that in this case the narrative was of my own past.

I don't really know just how our marriage would have played out if I hadn't ended up unconscious the next day from a terrible car accident I had on the way home after acing those four midterms I'd studied for. I remained unconscious for several days. Apparently, my head hit the windshield. I also broke five ribs and cracked my sternum. But more importantly, the accident put an end to my ability to live in continual cognitive dissonance. You might say it initiated a make-over of my brain.

The event itself is a hazy jumble – but in that haze, the outline of the story emerges. The last clear moment I remember occurred about five miles before the accident happened. In that moment, as I zipped through the rolling hills between Riverside and Beaumont at sixty miles per hour, high on life and my place in it, I had a sudden flash during which I fully understood the Meaning of Life. The Meaning of Life. Can you imagine? It had something to do with the grasses on the hills I was driving through.

I was driving smack into and against California's Santa Ana winds, the devil winds, as they are called here in the West. Beside me the hills were verdant green, marbled with red streaks from drying brome grass. It was all so incredibly lovely I felt like I might just levitate and drift off into the universe, car and all. It was then that some powerful feeling took hold me, and the grass itself, along with everything around me, revealed itself as the very meaning of existence. There didn't have to be anything beyond that. Definitely a had-to-be there experience of "isness." Yet even though I *was* there, I can't recall the actual content of that enlightenment specifically. Only the feeling it left with me.

Looking back now, it's easy to recognize my extreme hubris in believing for a second that any mere mortal could experience the meaning of existence, especially someone such as myself. Very un-Zen of me. But I *had* added the Romantic poets to the Metaphysical poets, had been flying high on Wordsworth and Coleridge, Keats and Shelly for two years. In short, I was primed.

The next foggy patch I remember is writhing in pain in a hospital. My VW bug convertible had plowed into and half-way under a maroon '55 Ford abandoned at the side of the highway, managing to carry the Ford 100 feet further down the road. Apparently, some heroic truck driver had extricated me and called for help. I didn't recall the '55 Ford until sometime after I woke up and Daryl asked if I knew what I'd hit. Then I saw that image clearly in front of me and described the car perfectly. Along with that memory came the feeling I'd had when I saw that Ford – that I was heading straight for it and that there was nothing I could do to stop it.

I remember, too, flashes of my own irrational behavior while the emergency doctors were examining me when I came in with the concussion, broken ribs, and cracked sternum. I had pulled two ligaments loose from my spine as well, one with a chip of bone. I recall that each time they asked me if I had any children, and they asked me several times, I went into a litany: Renee Debra, age 15, born April 28, 1958; Timothy Daniel, age 14, born, May 20, 1959, and so on until I had given the stats on all five of my children. Time and time again.

I also remember steadfastly refusing to give them a phone number so they could call my husband. I wouldn't even tell them his name. "Do you have a home phone number?" "Yes." "What is it?" I recall, and can still feel the sensory experience of moving my head continually from side to side against the pillow non-stop – partly because of the pain. Partly to emphasize my refusal. "I won't tell you." I remember saying again and again. "I don't want him to know where I am. He won't care." This went on for some time. Finally, I gave them the number of my friend, Diana, who now watched the children after school on Tuesdays and Thursdays. Then I remember nothing for a long time.

When I came to three days later, the room lay in a thick fog around me. I remember a nurse calling the doctor and then asking if I wanted to see my husband. "No. Why should I?" I remember saying. "He doesn't care."

The nurse looked shocked. She said that Daryl was right out in the waiting room with my sister Bobette. She would bring them in to see me.

When Daryl leaned down to talk to me, I suddenly felt like I might suffocate. "Get back," I told him. "You're breathing my air."

After he asked me if I knew what I'd hit, and I'd described it, I also remember him saying that my little VW Bug was mangled into a "pretzel," so mangled that "they couldn't tell if anything happened to the steering column."

I came home a week later, so weak and sore I couldn't pick up so much as an empty laundry basket for weeks. Glass slivers oozed out of my forehead for months. My children watched me with suspicion. I found out later that Daryl had told them I would become a "vegetable." He'd also said I'd been high on LSD when I crashed. These were the kinds of actions I was always discovering about Daryl. Of course, I hadn't been high on anything but life – and perhaps on acing the four mid-terms – but even if I had been, is that something a responsible parent would tell his children?

Actually, I didn't go straight home from the hospital. Instead, we all went to stay for two weeks with my mother at the Desert Mental Physics Center, where her new alcoholic husband was the grounds keeper. She had recently married the man who had briefly been married to Daryl's alcoholic mother before she died of a stroke at age forty-seven. Mother told me that the people at the spiritual center, people I'd never met, had been holding and continued to hold regular chanting vigils for me all the while I was in the hospital. They sent over special vegetarian foods for me while I was at mother's place. Except for occasional physical violence between my mother and her husband as they tried to kill each other after a couple of drinks, it was a very healing place to stay.

The accident had happened on May 1. It wasn't until May 22nd that I was actually back home in the house we were squatting in. On June 16th, Daryl left me for another woman, someone he'd been seeing before the accident and during the weeks I was recovering. June 16th was also the day I was bitten by a cone-nosed bug, commonly called a kissing-bug. For some time, I'd been allergic to the bug, a blood sucker that injects a blood thinner to keep the blood fluid. I turned bright red and began itching uncontrollably. Then I began to have trouble breathing, and had to have Daryl rush me to the emergency room yet again to be shot up with adrenalin to counteract my allergic reaction.

I returned from the hospital extremely woozy that day, still shaking from the shots – and wanted nothing more than to lie down on my bed and try to sleep it off. But no sooner had I hit the mattress than Daryl appeared at the bedroom door.

"I'm leaving," he said. "And I'm taking Renee and Timmy with me."

"I'm still loopy from the shot," I said, thinking he meant he was just going to town or something. "Can't you leave one of them here to help with Linda and Jimmy till I feel better? They're going to wake up soon. When will you be back, anyway?"

"I mean I'm leaving *you*." He turned and disappeared from the doorway.

"Leaving *me*?" I sprung up from the bed, adrenalin sending my heart into fury mode. "Not with Renee and Timmy!" I felt like I'd been hit by a truck. Glad as I was to have him go, I wasn't about to sacrifice my children so it could happen.

By the time I ran out to the car, all three of them were already inside it. He must have had them waiting there when he came in to tell me. Without a thought, I flung myself behind the back wheels of the car, shouting, "Over my dead body you're taking them!" I was at my best Nazimova self.

I was totally beside myself; it was as if I'd lost all my senses. I remember laying on the ground crying and screaming, and being totally out of control, which I hope was the result of my system being still in shock from the insect bite and all the adrenalin I'd been shot up with. And when I say I was beside myself, that is the position from which I remember being on the ground, as if I were standing there looking down at myself.

All my hysterics were to no avail, however. Daryl simple drove the car forward over the brush and rocks and down the hill through more brush and rocks to the dirt road leading to the highway, leaving me sobbing and broken-hearted over him taking two of my children.

After I'd lay sobbing on the ground for a time more, all the while knowing that I needed to go in and see if the kids were up from their nap, I finally opened my eyes. With my cheek still snug against the pebbled granite sand, I looked teary-eyed out at the world around me with pained and blurred vision. That's when I noticed that some of the pebbles in front and around me were hopping around. Something went quiet inside me. Forgetting my heartbreak completely, I sat up and rubbed my eyes, then stared back down at the ground. The pebbles were still hopping – not a lot of them and not very high. I lowered my face back down to ground-level to see this impossibility up close. What I realized after a few more moments of observation was that some of the pebbles were not pebbles at all but tiny hopping insects camouflaged to look exactly like pebbles.

The discovery seemed wondrous to me; this small miracle a window into a realm of promise that the Universe was working things out in its usual mysterious ways. I was suddenly filled with a profound joy that eclipsed the pain I'd been feeling – as if that pain had created a deep space in me that joy could now inhabit. Yet again, I had been saved by the wild. And I would return to those small rocks rising years later, finding in them a metaphor that served as title and theme years later for my first book of fiction. After observing the wonder a little longer, I got up and went in to check on my children.

Looking back now, I understand that from Daryl's standpoint, the drama of my kissing bug bite had almost upstaged the drama he had planned with his sudden departure. Taking Renee and Timmy might have been his way of making me care about him leaving at all – not that I needed to have been concerned, however, since he brought them both back two weeks later and dumped them off on my doorstep. They must have been more than his new woman wanted to deal with.

Despite the irrational, adrenalin-crazed behavior I exhibited when Daryl left with my children, the new post-accident me had already started to emerge. After the accident, I found that I developed a horrible headache whenever he was home, and one side of my head would go numb if I so much as thought about him, even while he was nowhere around. Something inside me had altered radically. The accident had also left me without fear – probably from amygdale damage. When I went through the *I Ching* to ask about the change in myself, I got an amazingly accurate description of a person being "constricted in the breath" who had an unbridled enthusiasm that needed to be channeled. As I read these words with tape wrapped tightly around my broken ribs, it was hard to ignore just how perfectly the metaphor matched both my mental and literal physical condition.

But I want to return to the issue of Daryl covered in dirt from, he said, "writhing and crying" in the driveway months ago "because he'd never again see my face when I looked at a flower." It has only been as I write this, some thirty-odd years later, that I also understand what Daryl might have been up to in that driveway. And might not, either. I'll never know for sure. The evidence is circumstantial but strong. A. I can't help connecting my vague memory of not being in control of my VW while it was heading for the maroon '55 Ford with (B.) Daryl's telling me why he'd come in covered in dirt. What else could he have been doing out there that made him sad, thinking about never seeing my face again?

And how can I not connect all that with Daryl telling me that the VW bug had been so mangled into a pretzel "that they couldn't tell if anything went wrong with the steering mechanism"? I hadn't asked him about it, hadn't even mentioned my not being able to steer the car away from the one parked on the side of the road. Why, then, did he volunteer that particular piece of information? Perhaps it's just a coincidence that the night before the accident he had been wallowing in the dirt in the same driveway where I parked my little bug. Perhaps his training a rifle sight on the woman he wanted out of the way years before had nothing to do with things. Nor did those pills I'd once found in my coffee cups, nor the mysterious and acute bout with food poisoning I'd had some years before. Perhaps it was really only those Devil winds that caused the accident.

Chapter Eleven
1973
The New Me Emerges

The accident, or the brain injury from the accident – or the revelation I had before the accident – had left me with much more than fearlessness and an inability to tolerate Daryl. It changed the way I saw my place in the universe. I remember a conversation I had with Bobette soon after Daryl left for good. We were in my summer bedroom, which was simply the open porch on the hill above the golf course. I had just captured a tarantula with a glass jar. While I'd been healing at the Mental Physics Center, the mice and tarantulas had completely taken over the house. Each spider I caught, I would let loose on the other side of town, next to an upper class neighborhood. I wanted the creatures to have a home with good prospects.

Bobette had driven up from LA to assure me that she had called and talked with each and every one of my professors, and that all of them had agreed to give me incompletes in my courses. That meant I had a full year to make up the incompletes by writing a final paper for each class. Bless her for her efforts, yet at the time the very idea of making up those incompletes seemed beyond the bounds of possibility. I could no longer read a word without getting an unbearable headache. And I wasn't sure that finishing those courses was what I was supposed to do now. I was convinced that I was supposed to be doing something different than what I had been doing. I had no idea what that something different was, but I was sure the Universe would soon show me what I was supposed to be doing.

"The universe has given me great gifts," I told Bobette. "Now it's time for me to give back to the universe. Time to earn those gifts."

I remember how astonished my sister looked when I said that. She surveyed the worn furniture around us, the curtainless window behind us in the house, and rickety chair she sat in. The lumpy mattress on the cement porch floor where I slept.

"Where?" She asked. "What gifts do you have? I don't see any great gifts. You don't have a damned thing."

I don't remember if I tried to explain it to her. Don't know if I could have explained the powerful conviction I now felt. It wasn't external or material gifts I meant, of course; I'd never been concerned with those kinds of things. And the gifts I spoke of went beyond any internal attributes as well – things such as intelligence, health, attractiveness, and strength. Beyond even the joy I'd received looking at clouds and flowers. It went beyond words as well. I'll never know just where the *I* that I knew as *me* was those days I wasn't conscious, but I came back not quite the same self. Some of the old self, too, of course, but I also came back someone else, someone who had been granted life for a reason that was still unexplained.

I realize there had to be a literal dimension to that feeling. Parts of my brain must have been injured, had perhaps even died. Perhaps I was now using sections of it that I hadn't accessed before. Structural change equals different self. But the quality of that different self can't be explained. It was as if something dormant in me had woken up. Suddenly just breathing the air was an astounding gift, to say nothing of having eyes to see the way light reflected off the leaves of the cottonwood next to the house, or having ears to hear to the whispering of those leaves brushing and slapping together in the breeze. In fact, with one notable exception, Daryl, everything was a miracle – though his departure certainly had been.

My sister, of course, was concerned about all the material absences in my life. As I look back, I can see that she had a point. I didn't see it then. Perhaps it was a good thing that I had lost all fear. There I was, squatting in a vermin-invested house, freshly abandoned with five children – Daryl had already dropped Renee and Timmy back off. I had no income and was

120

too weak and injured to work – and had glass slivers oozing out of my forehead daily. My only transportation was a barely running old Ford pickup that Daryl had practically demolished by crashing into dead *Tesota* trees to break the branches into fireplace-size chunks of wood. It had a difficult-to-engage clutch and stick shift, anyway, which made it too painful to drive with my fractured ribs. But none of these things concerned me. Instead, I was thrilled to be finally free. I felt more fully alive than ever. I was sure my new life would present endless opportunities to pay back the universe for the gifts it had given me. I could hardly wait to get started. Go figure.

The children and I remained in the house above the golf course for the rest of that summer, with field mice, pack rats and tarantulas multiplying daily. I remember hearing the creatures run across the big overhead beams at night, as if the beams were major highways in the village they'd made of our house. Sometimes I'd look up and find the creatures staring down from the ceiling beams during the day. And the rodents kept chewing apart the electrical cords on the fridge and lamps. Hairy black tarantulas, three inches across, could appear at any place at any time – I almost sat on one that had parked on the toilet seat. But it didn't cost me a dime in rent to live there, and money was what I didn't have.

Times might have been tough, but I was ecstatically happy – and oh-so-ready for my new life, convinced that I was secure in some great flow of universe that was taking me where I was supposed to go. My atheism had been tempered with brain change. Maybe not God, but the Universe would provide, and I wasn't about to let reality get in the way of its flow.

I'd had to modify my vegetarianism, at least until I had more resources for my family. After Daryl left, I borrowed back the rifle that I had given my brother to keep for safety's sake, which allowed me to walk back in the hills behind the house and shoot little miracles of life, aka rabbits and quail, for dinner.

The meat provided protein to go with all the saved up macaroni, rice and beans we lived on. I made all our bread. I couldn't grow a garden at that house because it cost too much. It was hard enough to pay a water truck to fill the tank once a month – so I started picking lambs quarters and pigweed and such for vegetables. Soon, however, we had no shortage of normal vegetables. Boxes of squash, zucchini, potatoes, tomatoes, and other assorted garden veggies began arriving on my doorstep every few days. My friend, Diana, was coordinating the overflow from people's gardens. For basic staples, I learned about a food surplus outlet that once a month gave out butter and huge blocks of processed cheese, as well as flour, sugar, dried milk and nasty-tasting canned meats to the poor. What else could we possibly need?

I'm not sure how well anyone could survive in such circumstances today. But it was 1973, and the country wasn't so mean then. In those days health, auto, and other insurances weren't required, and the state didn't subject those who didn't have insurance to dire financial penalties. Doctors' fees were more reasonable and they still made housecalls occasionally. They took payments, too – which meant families didn't have to spend their food and gas money to get their sick children treated. I didn't have to make payments for the hospitalization from my accident, fortunately, since I had been automatically covered as a full-time student. Students today get no such benefit without paying dearly for it, several thousand or more per semester. In those days, loopholes in the economic system still allowed folks to go through hard times without getting mired there permanently. My body was healing, although I was still tender around the ribs and had constant headaches, especially whenever I tried to read. Slivers of glass continued to ooze from my forehead. But by late fall, I had managed to write all the papers needed to fix my incompletes needed to get the B.A. in literature that I should have had in May.

Then a few hundred dollars arrived like manna from some

capitalist heaven, but really from a long overdue tax refund. Almost four hundred dollars. I cashed the check and stuffed the money under my mattress. Half belonged to Daryl, but I wasn't going to tell him. I figured he owed us. He hadn't provided a dime for Timmy and Renee when he returned them – nor for our other three. He never did cough up another dime for any of the children in the years that followed, not even after the judge in our default divorce ordered him to pay $60 per month a few months later. Yet his being simply being gone felt like pure wealth to me.

I soon decided to spend some of my mattress stash to move into a house in town and give the old house back to the creatures who dominated it. (I hadn't brought myself to kill the little deer mice, pack and kangaroo rats, or tarantulas. Killing animals for food to feed the children was one thing, but I wasn't willing to kill for simple convenience and we weren't willing to eat these things too.) The rent on the new house was $125 per month (in those days there was no requirement to pay both first and last months' rent, along with huge cleaning and damage deposits). Paying $125 in rent was bit scary after having paid none ($60 had been top rent for other places), but I figured I'd find a way to keep paying it. The Universe would provide. The big problem was how to move our stuff when I could barely lift the rifle to shoot those poor rabbits. But lo and behold, the Universe provided the muscular help I needed when an old friend – Lowell, who I'd known since high school – showed up in town to do the lifting and driving of the old pickup I still wasn't able to drive myself.

About three weeks after we moved, I found I could manage the gearshift on the old pickup. It was still painful but doable. This allowed me to apply for jobs. I got three local jobs right off, all part time. One was as a substitute teacher, thanks to my new degree (I had completed the papers assigned to finish my incomplete and had in hand a letter from the university saying I would have the official document soon), another was as a reporter on the town's weekly newspaper and the third job was as a weekend waitress at a fancy new restaurant and nightclub that had just opened in town – a quick cash job, although carrying trays of food was quite painful.

Childcare for short work stints was no problem. Renee, the oldest, was fifteen now, Tim fourteen, Kim, twelve, Linda eleven, and, Jimmy was turning nine. Besides, our new rental sat across the street from where my friend Diana and her children lived – and where she operated her babysitting business so the kids were over with her children a lot. I had never been so free.

Chapter Twelve
The Yellow Brick Road to Freedom

That fall, Gary and his wife, Joan, came by to help me with an aspect of my new life that was still missing, namely, a divorce from Daryl. I had picked up a do-it-yourself divorce form at the county office but couldn't translate the legalese on it enough to understand what the questions were asking. Even though I thought of myself as divorced, I knew it would be better to actually cut that legal tie. But the divorce form, short as it was, was not written in the literary language I understood, and its mysterious legalistic language about respondents and complainants had me stumped. I also didn't know how I would afford the $125 fee to get the thing filed in the first place, so I had pretty much decided that legality would have to wait.

But Gary and Joan had a plan. They said they would drive me to a commune in Indio, to see a legal-aid lawyer, Collin O' Donally, who lived there. They were going there as friends for a visit before backpacking through Europe but were sure he would also help me fill out the indecipherable form while we were there. A commune wasn't the usual place to do legal business but nothing about my life had ever been usual.

Actually, Gary had been telling me about this place for two or three years, even before we both transferred to the university in Riverside. Gary had told me I should meet the legendary Collin O'Donally, a legal aid attorney who was regionally famous for saving the poor from vicious landlords and other disasters. Actually, Collin had even been the attorney who finally saved some of us from being expelled for wearing black arm bands, although I never bothered to attend one of the Board meetings to meet our savior. Gary said Collin and another classmate of ours, Greg Butcherside, had recently co-formed a commune, partially based on what would today be called "sustainability." But I hadn't been impressed. The word *lawyer* was enough to make me turn my nose up at him.

Yet as a newly freed person, I now welcomed the chance to see what a real commune would be like. Communes, like the universities, were at the heart of the social movement I considered myself a part of. While I had wanted to attend the university to talk about ideas, another, more adventurous part of me wanted to be where the protest marches were happening. So an evening's adventure into a communal culture seemed delicious to me – and I might just get my divorce papers filled out while I was there meeting people who had pledged themselves to full-fledged "hippie" life. I was more than a little curious.

The first time I ever heard the term "hippie" had been about two years before I started college. Bobette's then-husband, Bob, looked at me one day and said, "Now I know what you are – a hippie."

"What's a hippie?" I'd asked. I had never heard the word before. At the time, we had neither a TV nor a radio. Rob must have been referring to my non-materialist orientation, my close-to-nature way of life. Or maybe it was my long hair and bare feet. It *was* a wild life I led, in terms of socialization at least. But I certainly wasn't a "peace, love, dope" type. Hippies were dropping out of a world I had never really been part of.

At any rate, in the years following that introduction to the word, I'd learned I did have a lot in common with the non-materialist hippies. In my reading I had come across the "Diggers" non-materialist philosophy – the real diggers, not the diggers from the summer of love – and I "dug" their philosophy. I had learned from attending school, too, that I did connect with hippie acid-head students – although acid was something I never tried. I figured I was already so open-minded about what constituted reality that I might just levitate off into space if I took acid. But I discovered a rare rapport with many of the former "acid -heads" I met at school, Gary being one of them.

So the mystique of that commune visit was tempered

slightly by the fact that I had learned from Gary that Greg and one other of the residents had been in my political science class at the community college before I'd transferred to the university. They, like I had, argued with instructor, and challenged the status quo, but I hadn't been impressed by their conclusions or the rationales they used. I considered both of them overly testosterone-based and brash, without much intellectual depth. But they *were* interesting young men, several years my junior, and definitely as radical as I was in their ideas. And they did seem to be walking their talk. According to Gary, the tall hairy giant, Greg Butcherside, was definitely the heart of the newly formed commune called Freeman's ranch. Apparently, Collin O' Donally, whom I hadn't yet met, was the brains.

It wasn't until we drove the sixty miles to Indio and were passing huge sand dune after dune, did I realize the appropriateness of the name, Freeman's Ranch. The name had come from Frank Herbert's sci-fi novel, *Dune*, where Freemen were the good guys fighting oppression on the planet Arrakis. We soon came to a thick tangle of ancient mesquite and turned off the pavement into a large area that the impenetrable circle of mesquite helped protect from sand blowing from the dunes, continuing down a long dirt driveway. The mesquite reminded me of a moat of bramble hiding the castle beyond in a fairytale.

We drove forward toward the hippie "castle" through the remains of an old grape vineyard, where rows and rows of crucifixes, remained peopled by gnarled vines that resembled mummified bodies hung on crosses. Naturally, to my literature-saturated mind, the rows of gnarled vines and the surrounding bramble moat hung heavy with symbolism. In fact, the entire world I inhabited at that time fairly dripped with symbolic significance, especially after the accident and brain makeover.

We parked at the bottom of a small hill below the long, white, many-roomed hippie house that spanned the top of the knoll. The knoll that the house had been built on had once been a sand dune, much like the ones beyond the perimeter of grape vineyard and mesquite moat, though it had long ago been stabilized. The symbolism of a house built on sand dunes managed to escape me, however. Instead, I was completely taken, lulled into a state of romantic reception, as if I had just entered into a literary fairy kingdom. I was more than ready to relax into the magic of it all.

Sun-browned bodies of various sizes and shapes swam and splashed in a homemade lake ringed with crab grass and shaded by tall poplar trees, whose hanging branches swayed in the breeze like Isadora Duncan dancing with her many scarves. Red-orange trumpet flowers and lavender wisteria wound their way up the white walls of the house. Bright bougainvillea splashed magenta everywhere, along with pink and white oleander hedges that bumped up against the moat of mesquite trees to help protect the compound. And all of this, every single bit, glittered gold with silica from the dunes beyond – and I would soon find out, would glitter silver in the full moonlight.

Inside the house, I found it impossible at first to keep all the names straight. The energy of the place burst though my senses. Everything seemed in constant motion. *Sergeant Pepper's Lonely Heart Club Band* blasted from speakers. Residents and guests stood around drinking beer, talking and laughing, playing pool in the big family room. Smoking dope, of course. Everyone seemed very hairy, the women with long hair and unshaved legs and underarms, the men with long hair, too, and beards, and heavily matted chests. The raucous energy of the place was infectious, the smell of sweat, grass and beer a fulfillment for my long-denied yearning for adventure. I flung my own long hair over my shoulder, sucked in a huge breath of the perfume, and reached for a joint.

This could be the turning point in the story where I shucked off my old life like the hair shirt it was and abandoned my own children to join these flower children. Lots of folks were doing that in those days. But I was not someone who could abandon her children, nor could I live without my hair shirt, for that matter. Wherever I went, I took both with me. (Well, I admit I *had* left the children with Diana for the night.) Besides, this was not that kind of a commune. Any flower children who wanted to live there had better be ready not only to plant their own flowers, but to harvest them for food as well.

The "hippies" at Freeman's Ranch, in fact, had planted large, lush gardens near the plastic-lined eco-pond out in the dry bed of dunes. The little lake was supplied with the appropriate fish and underwater plants. They had also put up corrals and barns that housed goats and pigs, chickens and geese. Vegetarians were in the minority, and the place was run by democratic vote. However, the name Free*man's* Ranch seemed especially appropriate for what looked to be a heavily male-dominated population, with several fewer women than men. There were a few children at the commune, too, ranging from age about six to teenage. Of course, it was hard that night to tell who actually lived there. That day, as on most days and evenings, Gary's friend Greg Butcherside explained, a constant stream of visitors flowed through, Gary, Joan and I being a case in point.

I had already learned from Gary how the wealthy owner of the place, a political radical himself, allowed the group to live there rent-free. That had come about because in the past the vacant old house had become infested with transient addicts who used it as a winter crash pad. The owner was an admirer of Collin O' Donally and his reputation for social justice, and Collin had convinced him that this new group of hippies would fix up, care for, and be an asset to his unoccupied property – which they indeed did and were. Collin even gave the place legal status as a non-profit school – which it soon became for real. Extremely non-profit.

While I was taking in all the boisterous activity, I happened to notice an odd-looking man laying on the carpet next to the far wall. Odd-looking in the context of the commune, at least, because he was clean-shaven and had not a strand of hair on his chest. None visible on his legs, either. And he appeared entirely naked except for a pair of ragged cutoffs. Somehow more naked than if he'd worn nothing at all. He reminded me of one of the naked baby packrats I had come across tucked in a cupboard back in our old house. This man is sucking in the energy of this place to sustain himself as surely as if he had an IV hooked up to it. Almost parasitically, I thought to myself. It creeped me out to watch him.

Sometime later, Gary and Joan reminded me of my purported purpose for our visit – actually their 'excuse' for bringing me so they could hang out at the place themselves – and took me over to where the legal expert was now sitting on the carpet at a low round table, part of the "floor-based furniture," along with the huge pillows scattered along the walls. The man they introduced me to as Collin O'Donally was the same man who I'd seen laying on the carpet earlier. He was now wearing a lavender dress shirt and sandals with his cutoffs, and the potent presence and charm of the man made a sizeable swipe across the blackboard of my memory, rendering my first impression faded and barely visible, though not erased entirely.

Collin stood to shake my hand. His gorgeous smile caught me off guard, as did his deep blue eyes, bright-lit with humor and intelligence. I describe them this way so I don't have to say they twinkled – but it seemed to me that they actually did. There was more than a little leprechaun in his expression as well. And his chocolate-colored hair, while shorter than the others', curled softly around his ears and neck, fell over his forehead when he turned his head. An Irish accent accompanied his colorful and articulate speech. It made me want to hear more. This was not what I had expected in an attorney.

If I *had* expected anything it would have been to put up with some dry and boring lawyer long enough to get the information I needed. Even though I'd never met a lawyer in my life, I was sure they had to be some stuffy, rigid, and logic-ridden species. Certainly I hadn't expected to find one so interesting and deliciously sexy. And Collin got even more interesting as the evening went on. Once we dispatched the legal issue and Collin let me know that, because of my low income, I could file the divorce papers for nothing, he gave me a tour of his art work, which turned out to be colorful oils and whimsical water colors, as well as murals on many of the commune walls. At some point he picked up a guitar and played and sang Johnny Cash songs.

We spent the next part of the evening sitting out on the sand dunes under the full moon. I listened, fascinated, as Collin told me about the sheer urban poverty he grew up in in Dublin, about dilapidated houses where sometimes families with twenty-five children shared one or two rooms and the entire floor of an apartment house shared one bathroom. His family was a small one, with only ten children. I remember scooping up handfuls of soft sand as we talked, watching the silver glitter in moonlight as it sifted through my fingers.

He told me how he'd became a flyweight boxing champion (I hated the idea of boxing as much as lawyering, but it all seemed part of an incredibly romantic past that made Daryl's past pale in comparison), how he'd immigrated to Canada to continue his career there, then immigrated here, joined the army and got his citizenship before studying law. It wasn't that all this spilled out from him without my coaxing. I practically had to interview him to get him to talk about himself.

I, on the other hand, giddy under the luminous moon and smitten by the moon-glitter silvering the dunes, spilled out my whole life story when he finished, then followed that up with my philosophy of life. When I told him how much I loved the Romantic poets, he began reciting from memory Wordsworth's and Byron's sonnets. From Byron, "She walks in beauty like the night/ Of cloudless climes and starry skies,/And all that's best of dark and bright./ Meets in her aspect and her eyes." And from Wordsworth, "She was a phantom of delight/ When first she came into my sight." Etcetera.

Be still my heart. Was there any better way to get my attention? I mean to *really* get my attention, down deep where it counts. I was already infatuated by the man's talents and accomplishments, especially after having been with Daryl for almost sixteen years. And those damned Irish eyes and ringlets of chocolate-colored hair. Worst of all, the musky smell of his sweat in the warm desert air was interpreted by my nostrils as perfume.

And now that I think back about it, something else happened while we were out on those moonlit sand dunes. I remember how a little black beetle scurried over the sand between us, leaving a trail of tiny prints across the dune. Inspired by the event, each of us came out with a few lines of poetry. Mine ended with something like "then a shiny black bug came out to say hello," while Collin's ended with "a shiny black bug went about minding its own business." Something in me took note.

In some strange way Collin's words shone a spotlight on the anthropomorphic and sophomoric nonsense of my own. That got my attention, too, and I appreciated the implied rebuke. This man had something to teach me.

Gary and Joan and I spent the night at the commune, and I remember how later, on my way to the bathroom, I saw Collin putting clean sheets on a mattress situated on the floor of his room (where I'd viewed some of his artwork). I remember also that a voice in me said firmly 'not tonight,' 'not yet.' So I went into the family room, bedded down beside my friends that night – and stayed there.

Already I was looking around, at least considering the other men that had been seeking me out. One of them was a hippie mechanic who lived and traveled in a wooden cabin he'd built on the back of a flatbed truck. He, too, painted and wrote poetry, although his talent in no way matched Collin's. He was almost foreign; his parents had immigrated from Russia, which gave him a lot of points with me, being that my favorite literary heroes were Russian. Best of all, he fixed up my old pickup for parts.

I'm embarrassed to admit it, but I had gone out to dinner with a deputy sheriff. I was intrigued because he was amazingly psychic and also very physical. Luckily, he lacked the language skills to deepen my interest. And both the sheriff and the hippie mechanic were eight years younger than I was. Collin appeared to be even younger, though, as I was to learn later, Collin was not always what he seemed and actually five years older than I was.

Soon after the visit to the commune, now with an actual degree firmly in hand, I applied for social worker jobs. The economy was in a recession in '73 but up popped two social worker jobs that I was invited to take a test for. One was in Riverside County, in Indio, the same county where Freeman's Ranch was located. The second job was back in the county where I lived, in fact, was in the town of Yucca Valley. The competition was tough during the recession for the one social work job in each county, but I aced the test and an interview landed me the job in Indio.

There was one slight problem: Indio was sixty-five miles from Yucca Valley, and I wasn't at all sure I wanted to move from the area where I had lived for so much of my life. I also had Diana right next door for free and willing babysitting at any time night or day. We had become like one family. And Yucca Valley was near the desert place my heart was rooted, which was the canyon that grew me. So I began commuting to the job in Indio, occasionally stopping by the commune for a quick visit on my way home. Sometimes I saw Collin, other times not.

Then one Friday, I arranged to have the children stay with Diana for an overnight. This freed me to spend hours out on the dunes with Collin. Gradually our philosophical and political discussions moved on to poetry and then on to consummate what the sweat-perfume had promised. It was a coming together more magical and fulfilling than I had imagined – a perfectly coordinated dance of sexual pleasure like nothing I had ever experienced before. Lust with poetry. I was quite impressed

Meanwhile, I had put yet another iron in the fire. Before I had actually started the social work job, I'd spent several days training in Riverside. While I was there, I'd called my favorite professor just to say hello. He invited me to have dinner with him and his wife. When I arrived, however, three other professors I had taken classes from (whoops – from whom I had taken classes) were there, and the professors actually provided me with one of those "very competitive" applications for a graduate fellowship that they had encouraged me to fill out earlier. "We can't promise anything, but we're all on the committee," they repeated several times. Their meaning was lost on me at the time. I thought they were just telling me not to get my hopes up. But I did fill out the application for them.

Only a few weeks into my new job in Indio, I had received a call from the social work office in San Bernardino asking me to come in for an interview, which I did. But since I had never heard back from them, I'd forgotten all about that job prospect. Yet not long after that magical night with Collin, San Bernardino called to say I was hired for that social worker position in Yucca Valley, and that I was, in fact, the only social worked to be hired that year in San Bernardino County. Now I had a real dilemma

I struggled mightily over the decision of whether or not to quit the job in Indio and take the one being offered to me in my old home town. It seemed obvious to me at the time that social work was my destiny. It was a way of giving back to the universe – and getting paid to do it. In other words, I could support my children and have health insurance while I did the

Universe's bidding. I liked the job in Indio but not the commute to get to it. I knew that eventually I would have to move closer if I stayed at the Indio job. My work in Indio allowed me to speak Spanish and work with Latino people, which was part of the reason I'd been hired. And of course working there let me spend time more with Collin. Things were developing between us – or was I reading too much into the moonlight conversations and poetry recitations that preceded the amazing sex? By this time I had discovered that, despite his appearance, he was five years older than I was, which made me take him more seriously.

On the other hand, my heart lived in white bread Yucca Valley, where at the time there were few Latinos around. But I had resources there. And, of course, my children were in school there. I had a hard time imagining all of us being happy living anywhere else. And I wasn't sure just what *was* developing with Collin in this era of free love and didn't think I should base my decision on what might or might not develop with him in the first place.

I suppose it was partially a matter of territory as well. I also was uneasy, I realize now, about going to live in Collin's territory, the low desert commune, even if things did develop. The wild high desert was my home ground. When I'd lived with Daryl on his turf, the city he'd grown up in, I lost myself. It was only by bringing him onto my home ground, back to the desert, that I regained the power to become myself again. Like my mother not wanting to leave her beloved canyon, I knew best who I was when I was on the land that was part of me, was bonded with the wild place that grew me.

On yet another level, I'd never had much experience at making positive decisions. More like zero experience. Up to this point in my life, any choices I *had* made had been a matter of choosing between the less bad option of several terrible options. I was completely new at making decisions between favorable options. Most of my life I had simply reacted to situations as they came up. I had "decided" to go to college – but not in any conscious and rational way. As I've said, I wasn't even sure the concept of conscious decisions was actually real. And since my accident and the brain injury, I had experienced myself as caught in some great cosmic flow. Now I had two flowing rivers in front of me and no clear sign of which flow to go with – the one maybe leading to Collin, or the one keeping me in my heart's place. In that regard, the job popping up in right there in Yucca Valley seemed to be a sign that I should stay right there where I was.

I took the new job in Yucca Valley.

My life as a social worker couldn't have been more different than my life as a student. I had traded the world of ideas and mystical literary speculation about the meaning of the universe for the nitty gritty world of helping people survive the lives they'd been trapped in. I found I was as good at doing that as I had been at juggling ideas and writing papers – maybe because I'd had do much experience doing that myself. And the results were much more tangible. Never before had I had any power to manipulate "the system." As a professional, I now had access to power and resources I could use to help people who needed them. I grew heady with these new powers and used them to the max. Some would say abused. I gave my anarchistic soul its head and manipulated rules whenever I needed to to help my needy clients. I'd always had disdain for rules. Most societal rules, I believed, had been made to oppress people. I knew whose side I was on and used the rules to unoppress people. I saw myself as a warrior of and for the people.

Officially, the job called for me to use a "matrix" to help others help themselves. The underlying premise of that matrix was that clients had been stupid and helpless their whole lives and that was why they needed help. Total bullshit, I thought. At least for those clients who lived there in that tough-to-survive desert during that time. Sure some were. Others were ill or mentally ill or dealing with aging and fading minds. Yet most just plain needed help to get through a period where their lives had fallen apart. In my view, they needed someone who cared to tell them they *could* do it and to help them get to a better place. Because I had been poor and was even then still a single mother with five children ages nine to sixteen, I was one of them and I let them know it.

It's hard to explain how effective I was at the people helping part of my job. (When it came to the paperwork part I eschewed, not so much) But anyone working with me at the time would verify my passion and effectiveness. The eligibility workers who actually doled out the money, however, were wary of me. Lucky for me, the woman in charge of the entire county social work department, the woman who'd hired me and told me about the matrix, was also an anarchist of sorts. I remember the time the two of us were having lunch in a small cafe one afternoon when it was 117 degrees outside. When we'd parked in the parking lot, we noticed an animal control truck already parked in the lot and could hear the dogs inside whining and crying as we walked by. Inside the restaurant, the animal control officer was laughing and joking with restaurant staff as he sat with his lunch at the counter. This continued all during our lunch and I remember both she and I kept glancing out the window where the animals were trapped and suffering in the back of the metal truck. When we finished lunch and walked out toward the county car, the two of us looked at each other, walked over to the control truck where the poor dogs were now whimpering weakly, unlatched the metal back door, and swung it open to let the dogs run free. Neither of us said a word.

My immediate supervisor was based in San Bernardino, as was the woman in charge of everything, and only showed up occasionally to check on things. That pretty much gave me free reign to accomplish the job anyway I needed to – which suited me perfectly. When destitute single mothers were camping on the desert with their children and couldn't get help because they didn't have an address, I found one for them. Either we "used" an address or I moved them into my backyard, or into a friend's backyard, or into Black Canyon Campground, which actually collected mail for its campers and cost only $2.00 a night. In short, I did whatever was needed to get them the help to have their own place.

I started a "help-yourself" fruit and vegetable stand in my front yard, driving the county car in early morning down to the weigh station in the low desert, where I loaded up all the excess fruit and vegetables that trucks abandoned, thereby rescuing the produce from the hot sun and making it available where it was needed. On weekends, I rounded up friends to help me move elderly clients from little cabins out on the desert into town where they would be closer to resources.

When I saw how often errant husbands managed to move back into homes and families they had abandoned, then emotionally and/or physically abused their wives and children, ruining the little family's fragile new start, I started a do-it-yourself divorce service. This meant providing forms and helping women to fill them out, including the low income waivers that allowed them to file for free. I even took the forms into the county seat for them. When clients had life complications that didn't fit on the rigid forms – which was often – I phoned Collin for advice.

I was seeing Collin regularly by that time. Sometimes he would find a way up to Yucca Valley, but more often I loaded up the kids in the pickup and took them down to the commune, where they swam in the little lake and just hung around. Sometimes they worked in the garden, or helped feed chickens and pigs, or milked goats. Food preparation was nearly constant there and the girls learned to make tortillas by hand, as well as start simple cheeses. My children loved the place and the commune folks loved my children – and kept them occupied. That way I could be out on the dunes at night with Collin while he recited more lines from Wordsworth, Byron and

Shelley. Often he would add to the romance by putting on records like Handel's *Two Oboes and a Continuo* or Barber's *Adagio for Strings* from his classical record collection and blasting music out into the midnight air on the commune's giant speakers. We would sometimes fall asleep on the soft dunes, wrapped only in lovely notes

These were heady times for me at work and play. Far too heady. After all those years of powerlessness, my head ballooned up, made me giddy, warped my perspective. I was no humble Mother Teresa. I had read *Dune*, the book that had inspired the name and concept of Freeman's Ranch. And I had identified as well – but not with the Freemen. My identification was with the main character, Paul, who had the ability to absorb the poison excrement of the sandworm and transform it into psychic energy. Psychic power, actually. At the time that seemed to me an apt metaphor for what I was doing as a social worker. I saw myself as listening to and absorbing the pain and misery, the craziness and negativity of many clients who came in and transforming all that into the power to help them. I developed delusions of invulnerability.

I was somewhat alarmed the first time one of my clients, a young single mother named Charlene, came in and said she just needed to touch me. She said that just touching me would empower her to get through the day. That made me uncomfortable, but I gave her a hug and sent her on her way. The second time, when another came in and client said and did nearly the same thing, it really gave me pause. It reminded me too much of the movie *Jesus Christ Superstar*, which I had recently seen, where the sick and the lepers tried to touch the Great Healer as he walked by. A more reflective person might have done more than I did – which was to simply wonder what was going on and decide to be more careful with whatever energy I seemed to be sending out.

Somewhere around this time, I remember that it was May, just before the kids got out of school, my landlord sold the house we were living in. We were given thirty days notice. For three weeks I scoured Yucca Valley to find another place to live, one that I could actually afford. With the housing shortage that had developed, there were no affordable houses to be found, especially in such a short period of time. There weren't even any unaffordable houses available. Meanwhile, our new friends at the commune had been begging us to move in there long before the thirty day notice came. The kids were sold on the idea. All these factors seemed to point out a different direction of flow from the universe – one that led straight to the commune. I finally relented – but just for the summer. I wasn't comfortable with such a radical move being permanent for my family. My plan was to commute to Yucca Valley to work and when school started, we would move back. Surely a house in Yucca Valley would be available by then.

It seems likely as I write this that on some level the warrior self I exercised at work had to be in conflict with my newly found 'go-with-the-flow-of the-Universe' self. The warrior me that 'conquered' rattlers had been fully freed to do battle for the good in my social work. It seemed more in tune with my core nature than going with the flow, which was a concept I had only recently realized played a powerful part in the way things worked. I don't remember being conscious of this at the time. Even today, I still struggle with finding a balance between these somewhat opposite elements, with knowing when and where I need to stop and do battle, and when and where I need to stay open and receptive to synchronistic possibilities that often manifest themselves as part of a problem.

Chapter Thirteen
The Chasm between Magic and Reality

Freeman's Ranch, with all the grounding in its gardens and farm animals, appeared seductively wholesome. At the same time, it felt like some magical, mystical place outside of time. It was difficult for anyone who visited Freeman's Ranch, including myself, not to feel as if the place was the center of some timeless and yet contemporary universe. My move there was like entering into that mythological world, spending each and every day smack in middle of a labyrinth of symbolism. Much like my own literature-patterned brain; my eyes looked out on a world saturated with symbolic significance.

One thing I had in common with Freeman's Ranch residents, at least with the movers and shakers, was that, in a way, we were all refugees of literature. Just as Steinbeck's *The Grapes of Wrath* and *East of Eden* had informed my own early choices, and Freeman Ranch had been founded on ideas from Frank Herbert's *Dune,* concepts from Castaneda's and Tolkien's work crept into every family discussion and decision as well. Dill was big on *Stranger in a Strange Land.* Collin himself grew up on *Les Miserables* and *Germinal.* Those were forms of the literary language I spoke as well.

However, Freeman's Ranch literary language and thinking had been greatly informed as well by contemporary music, thought, and the events of the 'happening' '60's era – aspects that, because of my isolation, I had only recently encountered. My own thinking at the time was more an eclectic mix of ideas from Jung, Freud, Sartre, deBeauvoir, Camus, Marx, Trotsky, Dostoevsky, Dickens, Godwin, Kropotkin, and countless others that commune members hadn't read. And, of course, I also walked around with lines and concepts from the Romantic and Metaphysical poets, namely, Wordsworth, Coleridge, Keats, Shelly, Byron, Donne, Trahern, Vaughn, Herbert (Not Frank, but George) infusing my heart and spirit choices.

I moved my family into the commune for the summer with some excitement, but on a more practical level, with considerable trepidation. It was only for the summer, I kept reassuring myself. Before the move, I had been more than satisfied living on the edge of the edge of the social change that I was so attracted to. I'd been accepted as part of the Freemans' Ranch family, yet had remained on the periphery, allowing me to continue to enjoy stability and empowerment in my other life for the first time. It had been the best of both worlds. My eight-thousand-dollar a year salary as a social worker seemed like a fortune in 1974. Plus health insurance. All this while helping people get back on their feet.

I finally had some control over my own life, could set my own rules. My children's ages now ranged from ten to sixteen, which in itself had set me freer than I had ever been. The child-raising years that had begun when I was sixteen finally began to fade, would soon be a part of the past. My real life was beginning at age thirty-three.

Yet, as I said earlier, the "family" philosophy of "dropping out" of the main culture wasn't a concept I could relate to. I'd never had a bourgeois past to drop out of, had never really been a part of the mainstream, so the idea of living an isolated, sustainable, and self-sufficient lifestyle was the last thing I wanted at the time. Been there, done that – in Pipes Canyon. I knew where that led. Nowhere. Like others in the commune, I wanted to shuck off my past, except that my past life in Pipes Canyon seemed to be the life they wanted to find. Well, that's a bit of an exaggeration, but close. My own family's lifestyle in Pipes Canyon developed out of a need to survive. It hadn't been a conscious choice to reject the dominate culture, which was what the founders of Freeman's Ranch wanted to do. Although my mother had once sought independence from societal norms, by the time I came into being, that desire had faded, and my family remained on the periphery of the local and larger community, as unconventional as that desert community was.

And, after all, my dad painted buildings for Hollywood for a while. Actually, the group at Freeman's Ranch worked in that 'outside' world, too, bringing in cash by working as gardeners and doing general clean-up for the rich in Palm Desert. Collin occasionally took court cases for pay – usually drug-related cases.

The drug use at the commune bothered me, too, even though the "family" there assured me that my children would be banned from any drugs. It wasn't so much the ubiquitous use of grass around the place. Smoking grass was the sacrament of the social revolution. I took hits when I was there, as I had occasionally with Gary. It was fun but not something I looked forward to. Yet I knew that acid and schrooms occasionally hit the scene, as they did everywhere then. That interested me, but it wasn't something I wanted to do or to have my children involved in.

Beer was big as well with many folks at the commune, too, but shunned by others. My experience with alcohol - except for my one-night stand with vodka at seventeen, and the thirtieth birthday party where I drank a bottle of Annie Greensprings, then climbed up a table to do rooster crows and other animal sounds as a part of "Old MacDonald's Farm" - was confined to sipping at a single glass of white wine with ice cubes all evening at parties a few times in my life.

In short, Freeman's Ranch was not a place I would have sought out to live permanently, but it did seem like a place for an interesting summer adventure. Especially since the flow of the Universe seemed to be guiding me straight for it.

A brief cast of main characters in my new "temporary" family: Of course there was Collin, who I've already said was the brains of the place. Then there was Greg, the heart – a talented hippie from redwood country whose vision was getting off the grid – growing the animal and plant food for the Freeman's Ranch members and eventually powering up the place with methane from human and animal waste. Maybe the soul of Freeman's Ranch was Dill, so called because he looked a little like Bob Dylan. He sang a little like him, too, except off key and without a smidgen of genius. He was also a trust fund grandson of the National Geographic family clan.

The women, Madge and Marda, Latina sisters, and to some extent Cathy, had to be the guts of the place. They worked in the garden, prepared the food, did laundry – and generally took care of the physical needs of the place, including I was later to learn at times the sexual needs of the males. Sound familiar? The family belief, however, was that the women were doing these things out of complete sexual and political freedom. Maybe that was true – yet I didn't believe it for a minute. Of course, I didn't have a complete handle on the dynamics of their true role when I moved in – I supposed I'd been spending too much time focused on Collin to dig beneath the romantic and sometimes magical-appearing surface – but it didn't take me long to figure it out once I moved in.

Five other males, a pair of twins among them, two other women, three teen-age males, Randy, Silacyb, and Josh, a sixteen year old girl, and Madge's father, Tom, were also residents, at least part-time. Then there was Madge's six-year-old daughter, Sigh, and Collin's precocious eleven-year old daughter, Tara. It would be too confusing to go through all twenty residents, person by person, though each one of them, no matter what age, played a powerful role. When I arrived with my little brood, the Freeman Ranch population jumped to twenty-five.

The day I moved in, I was surprised to find a couple hundred Buddhist Monks camped on the grass around the lake. Who knows why they had made the notorious Freeman Ranch a stop on their peace march to Washington, but that was the way the place worked. I can still picture those hundreds of tangerine-robed men lounging on the grass around the lake and on the dunes beyond as I drove up, my pickup piled high with furniture and other possessions. It was the first of three pickup

144

loads – a commune pickup and a friend's truck drove in right behind me. Several monks walked up to help us unload. I breathed in the smell of barbeque, wisteria, goat, pig and chicken from the corrals, and grass of both kinds – then stepped smack into the 'happening-center of the universe' for my summer adventure.

A few of my personal belongings went into Collin's room with me. Collin was one of few residents with enough status to have a room of his own. Most of the several bedrooms had multiple occupancy, partitioned off with cotton tapestries, and several residents floated and had no permanent place. My children scattered out among the rooms, eager to become as truly communal as anyone else there. Actually, Timmy, my oldest son hadn't come with us. I had agreed to let him stay with his best friend's family for the summer. Even at fifteen, he was still the "straight one."

The deal that the Freeman Ranch family had agreed upon concerning my possessions was that my fridge, washer, sofa, dishes, pots and pans and various essentials would go onto a slab and be wrapped with tarps so not to meld into the rest and become communal. That way they wouldn't be hard to extract when I left in the fall. Beds and dressers and personal possessions would be moved into the house but would remain ours as well when we left. It wasn't that anything my kids and I possessed was valuable. The sofa had been given to us, had, in fact, appeared magically on our doorstep when we returned home one day. The fridge was a cast-off from friends, as were dressers and beds, pots, pans and dishes. I'm not even sure anything except our clothing had actually been purchased – and that from thrift stores. Still, that fact made everything we had seem even more valuable. Besides, how in the world could I ever replace it all?

Sexually speaking, those first few weeks were the happiest of my life. Collin and I spent much time, you might say, attending to such matters. That first night, after a few bouts of love making, Collin and I slipped stealthily out to the lake with signs he had painted the morning before I arrived and planted them by the shore where the monks slept. The signs read: *Walking on Water Prohibited* and *Please Don't Walk on the Water.* It didn't seem to matter that the joke-metaphor mixed religions. The monks remained around a few days, earning their keep by picking up trash on the roads leading to the commune. I remember that they also shored up one side of the sand dune hill the communal house had been built on, shoveling back by hand the sand that had started slipping away. I was still too deep in the romance of the place, too full of the language of poetry and symphonies in the night, still too sticky with sex to plumb that metaphor.

Not that I was free to become fully immersed in the place. Five days a week I made the hour each way commute to Yucca Valley and spent from 8:00 am to 5:00 pm in my position as a social worker. So I still had one foot firmly planted back in the life I had begun to create for my new self, but could also enjoy the long summer evenings and weekends with Collin.

I remember that summer at Freeman Ranch as a blur of sex, poetry, nights with Collin out on the dunes, and numerous moonlight swims in the lake. Days brought non-stop visitors, frequent communal barbeques and parties attended by 'family' members and friends. And it was hot, hot, hot down there in the lower desert in summer, sometimes close to 120 degrees. Once it even reached 125. It was extremely humid as well because of agriculture in the nearby Coachella Valley. Sometimes commune residents would just pile into vehicles, head for the mountains surrounding the valley, and camp out under trees until the weather cooled.

It didn't take long before the romance of communal living wore thin, though. The problem with the place was that it was full of human beings dealing with the issues of day to day living. There were constant democratic debates among family members, some of them quite heated, concerning each and every detail of daily life: What kind of dish soap to use, how much to use, and how much rinsing of dishes needed to be done (usually argued by males who did no dishes). There were on-going arguments over the effect of slightly old vegetables on the human body, over the effects of meat of any kind on the human body and on the environment, arguments about which kinds of vegetables should be planted next to each other and why, about when to pick said vegetables, more arguments over whether it was ethical for humans to kill the animals they raised (applied specifically to the animals raised at Freeman's Ranch), over toilet paper and toilet flushing, over electric lights versus candles, over the use of the one air-conditioning unit that sometimes worked to cool the big family room, over the social meaning of music (Collin's elitist classical music that was written at the expense of the down-trodden versus the Beatles, Dylan and other socially conscious and progressive folk music), over whether or not Dylan had sold out in Newport, over various kinds and levels of drug use, over similar alcohol issues. Frequent and lengthy philosophical disagreements broke out over whether "gathering" various metals lying around rich businesses and selling said metal was actually a heroic act against the bourgeois or simple theft, over whether or not to open the place up to any and all visitors the Universe led there – and endless arguments over who said what to whom last Thursday (family meeting day) and why.

I was able to avoid much of this non-stop democracy by my going to work five days a week. The two hours of commuting time (one each way) helped keep me out of it as well. It wasn't long before I became aware of how much better I felt when I was away from the place. And how, when I returned, my own thinking and being became mired in some thick swamp of communal thought and energy. Having spent most of my childhood in that isolated canyon, and all of it with a mother I had to protect myself from, I had learned to decide things for myself, and often for my younger sister and brother. out of necessity. Even in my marriage to Daryl, I'd become the major decision maker, which is the way I'd managed to get myself back to and through school. So my background did not much prepare me for communal politics or for living quarters with a semi-stable and somewhat adolescent population of twenty-five. And I had no desire to participate in discussions about trivia that seemed to me to be an utter waste of time. I became even gladder that I was only there for my 'summer vacation.'

Even so, Collin and I shared many good times. He was, of course, the main reason I'd been so willing to follow the Universe's seeming dictate that I move down there for the summer. That and my children's enthusiasm for the place. And my own sense of adventure – even if it had faded rather quickly. The physical place itself had also drawn me. I loved the glittering chips of mica fool's gold from the dunes that permeated everything. Mica simply could not be washed from clothing, even with my hearty little Maytag washer that I had purchased from my mother when my youngest was born ten years before. The washer had been adopted into the Freeman family when their old washer broke down a week after I moved in. Mica glittered from every window ledge and floor, from the leaves of trees, and from blossoms of fuchsia bougainvillea, scarlet trumpets, and purple wisteria outside my bedroom window – I mean Collin's bedroom window. But I loved seeing its golden shimmer on Collin's skin, on my own after poetry and sex on the dunes. Loved seeing the light gold dusting on the sunbaked naked bodies of children as they swung out over the lake on a rope that hung from Isabella, the poplar tree, and splashed down or slid smoothly into the water.

Yet even with the lake, the oppressive heat drove the family to escape the place. I remember, in particular, one camping trip some of us made that summer. It was a trip to the family homestead in Pipes Canyon. The group was eager to experience the wild nature that I'd grown up in. Most of the group members didn't actually camp but slept inside the old cabin, since Mother wasn't living there at the time. In fact, the cabin had remained empty for most of the time after my parents' divorce. The place was pungent with rodent urine. I wasn't about to sleep inside.

The next morning, after a campfire breakfast of cheese melted over scrambled eggs and popcorn potatoes, I took the group on a hike up the canyon to show them a ridge that led into a bigger canyon that had at its end a small waterfall and swimmable pool of water. That watery canyon was one of my favorite places. It also had gooseberry bushes where bears sometimes came to eat. The place was several miles away and entailed a very steep hike up a mountain, without any trail except those made by various animals. If the group wanted to see wild nature, well, that's what I would show them. We didn't make it very far into the wild, however, before someone in the group spotted a rattler and bedlam broke out.

Everyone started shouting out *power meat*! *Power meat!* It was straight out of Castaneda. I, myself, had been experiencing intense macha as I showed off the homestead and my old stomping grounds in the wilderness. That, of course, included showing off how tough I was. Tougher than any of *them*! So when we saw the snake and everybody started freaking out about power meat, my macha went into high gear. I grabbed up a branch from a dead Manzanita and went after the poor snake, which was trying its hardest to crawl away and escape the frenzied maniacs. Swell-headed from demonstrating my prowess, I sawed the snake's head off with the branch even as someone was trying to hand me a pocket knife.

But this snake wasn't destined to become one of my hatband badges of courage. That would have meant taking the dead rattler back to the cabin, locating a board, nails and hammer and carefully skinning it. What this group wanted from the creature was, of course, power meat. I, therefore, stripped the scaly skin from the poor snake roughly and rudely, then gutted and washed the bony carcass. Meanwhile, some members of our little snake-thirsty mob had built a campfire. The reptile was then unceremoniously strung up with a strand of rusty bailing wire between two crude poles placed on either side of that fire and roasted even before the last of its reflex spasms had quit.

Now I've said I was not a stranger to rattlesnake meat. I'd eaten it a couple of times breaded and fried it up in sections. The meat tasted a little like chicken, only chewier and with a acid tang to it. Not too bad when cooked right, but I didn't particularly like it. Besides, it was chock full of tiny bones.

I warned the group that this was no way to cook a rattler, but some kind of rabid group-think had taken hold. A zealous throng created by the pages of Castaneda's fiction. It wasn't long before someone pulled the power meat from the fire and everyone fought like hell to get themselves a chunk of it – even some of the vegetarians. The texture fell somewhere between rubber and electric wire, the taste about the same, so nasty I felt like I was eating vulture meat. I spit it out, but the others managed to choke enough down so they felt transformed into powerful and mystical beings who then went primal around the campfire for several hours. Some of them, I suspect, had consumed substances other than power meat as well. Sick at heart over my part in all this, I parked myself on a rock and watched the spectacle, understanding, once my macha had calmed, that the only wild nature that interested the group was created by words and existed only in their own heads. It was nothing like the actual wild I knew, which we never made it to.

My summer of freedom and adventure soon came to an abrupt end, however. By late August I began to suspect that my IUD had failed. Perhaps Collin and I had tested it once too often. It had been on my birthday in early August that I'd first felt the queasiness. It had to be the smoked oysters I'd eaten, I told myself, and found excuses for several other episodes of a certain kind of nausea I hadn't felt for almost eleven years. And even after the pregnancy was confirmed at the end of the month, I kept thinking – and hoping wildly – that I might just wake up and find I was only trapped in some kind of nightmare. That this nightmare of another pregnancy after all this time wasn't my real life. It couldn't really be happening, could it? Whenever I was caught in a bad dream as a child, I would crawl into a pillowcase and chew my way out of one of the far corners. The method never failed me until now. There was no dream pillowcase to be found out there in the real world.

I don't think anything had ever hit me as hard. Until this point in my life I'd found it natural to adjust to the constant stream of life events – pregnancies, Daryl's cheating and lying and destructive behaviors, to his psychotic episodes. That was the way life worked. My life anyway. I deflected what I could, accepted and made necessary changes to accommodate what I couldn't change. Which was most things. I would simply come up with plans a, b, c, etc., and go on with my life. And I had done it without any of the dark feelings that were overwhelming me now. After all, celery always floats. Doesn't it?

But now I had not only glimpsed the light at the end of the tunnel, but had actually stepped out into that light for short periods of time. In the past, I doubt I even knew there was light outside my tunnel. I had just adjusted to varying shades of darkness as if it were the natural state of things – which in those days it had been.

Well, that might be going too far. I had always known that light was there – even if it wasn't meant for me. Actually, I had seen it in hundreds of books, in the ideas and lives in those books. Perhaps that had kept me from feeling mired in the lack of light in my own life. All around me, the celery was still floating, the sun was glancing off pine needles, and when it wasn't, clouds were making magical shapes overhead – if they weren't raining, and I loved rain. I loved the natural world around me. That was always what mattered. But after having been out in the light of freedom and away from my tunnel for a few visits, I wanted more of what I'd found out there, more freedom to follow my own inclinations. The idea of being pregnant again put me solidly back inside that tunnel, far away from the opening, and wrapped chains around my legs to keep me there. The light became a tiny pinhead glow off in the distance, with iron bars slapped in front of the exit.

I hadn't had to worry about pregnancy for some time. Soon after Jimmy, our fifth, was born, Daryl had gotten a vasectomy. Before that my body had managed to outsmart every birth control device available at the time. When we split up, I went on the pill, but changed to an IUD after the pill put boils on my rear. Now my fertile body had found a way around even that device.

I thought seriously about abortion, which had become a legal option the year before with Roe v Wade. In fact, the gynecologist I went to was known around town as "that abortion doctor." Collin said it was totally my decision, that he would rather I have the child and would accept responsibility as the father, but that he would also accept whatever decision I made. I *so* didn't want another child, and I was absolutely pro-choice. At least for other people. It would be so easy to simply have the protoplasm sucked right out of me. But I'd birthed too many children to be able to think that what was inside me was simply a blob of protoplasm. I knew, if undisturbed, that it would become a being. It was a being-in-formation, and seemed to be a determined one that managed to get through all the protection I had in place. Somehow it didn't seem right for me to simply decide it would never become. After all, I wouldn't even kill flies and spiders unless I were going to eat them (and so far that hadn't come to pass). How was I to kill the possibility of a soul's coming to be?

Also, as Superwoman, I knew there was no question that I couldn't take care of another child, no matter how disturbed I felt about having it. The same over-confidence complex that made me a super social worker, that had made me a super student in the middle of my complicated life, now assured me that I hadn't the option of an excuse. If I killed the child's possibility for life, it would be simply for my own convenience. And I didn't think the Universe had graced me with the gifts it had without expecting some extra responsibilities. I was supposed to be giving back to the Universe for those gifts. In what way was an abortion giving back? (The rationale of overpopulation didn't occur to me.) I also had qualms about fighting the flow of a Universe that had provided me with the abilities that were carrying me into a new life. It appeared that the same flow was showing me I would need to take another child with me into that new life.

I did have one out, though. My doctor assured me that pregnancy and birth were much safer without the IUD left in place, yet that there was a substantial risk that removing an IUD would also remove the pregnancy by miscarriage. It was my last hope. I didn't believe that having the IUD removed for safety sake would be fighting the flow of the Universe, and it just might end the nightmare of the pregnancy. A way of asking the Universe, "did you really mean it?" I sure hoped not.

I lay on the examination table, my feet trapped in metal stirrups, hoping this safety precaution would free me. Yet all I felt was a tiny pinch when the doctor reached in and pulled out the IUD. "The device was perfectly in place," he said. "There's no reason it should have failed." But I knew why the perfectly-in-place device had failed. Whoever was inside me really wanted to come into this world. The Universe had now decreed it. Who was I to say no?

Chapter Fourteen
Barefoot and Pregnant Again

When I left the doctor's office that day, my dillusional superwoman-self felt as if she'd been coated with Kryptonite, then shot out of the sky with a cannon and plummeted to earth. I went home battered and concussed from thudding into the ground – as dizzy and off balance inside emotionally as I had been physically after my accident. Why was this happening now, just when I almost had a life? How was I going to give back to the Universe in this shape? The doctor had said I was three months plus along, which didn't make sense since I had just missed my second period.

My plan before the doctor's verdict had been to look for a house back in Yucca Valley. I'd been holding off since the queasiness started, had gone into some kind of action-paralysis – even though I knew the kids would need to start school in mid September. That meant I had to get moving. But *now* what were my options? Would I even be able to continue working as a professional social worker while pregnant and unmarried like many of the clients I helped?

I talked with my supervisor when he made his rounds in Yucca Valley, told him I was pregnant but wanted to keep on working. He said I could work pregnant as long as I wanted, that what I did on my own time was my own business. He turned a little red when I assured him that I had indeed gotten pregnant on my own time.

Meanwhile, folks at Freeman's Ranch were turning up the pressure for me to stay put. I shouldn't move back to Yucca Valley pregnant, they argued. Who knew how long I could keep working? Wouldn't it be easier to raise the child communally – and didn't the child belong to the commune, too, since I'd gotten pregnant there?

Collin had long ago made the Ranch legally accredited as the School of the Dunes. He said it would be easy to fire up the school for real for my children, as well as for the others living there. It would be an alternative school, with commune members all contributing by teaching from subjects they had skills in. He could teach history and democratic process, Greg was a math whiz, I could teach literature and writing, and so on. We could enlist the older children to teach basic skills to younger children, which would be good for both. Since I had attended a one-room school grades one through three, I knew the strengths of that system. And I did like the idea of controlling and integrating the curriculum in radical ways. For instance, I could see the kids having a quasi-Spanish immersion by attending the informal classes I was already teaching migrant workers one night a week. We could make field trips to various places to make the children's learning more real and experiential.

Naturally, my children were enthusiastic about the idea of staying. They had wanted to stay at Freeman's Ranch forever and hadn't wanted to leave in the first place. Now they were excited by the prospect of the alternative school as well. Although the ideas I held were radical, applying those ideas to my children's actual lives was being tested. This was not some summer adventure we were talking about. I was wary of making such a drastic change concerning the children's education, one that might harm them when we did go back to the "real" world of the mainstream. And Timmy would not be with us. The family he'd been staying with in Yucca Valley were more than happy to let him remain with them for his last year of high school. Yet actually making the final decision seemed impossible. I seemed to have entered some great cloud of confusion and had lost all capacity to think clearly in my murky emotional state. There seemed to be no good solution as long as my being pregnant was a factor in it. And as much as I fought that fact, it didn't look like it was going to change. I knew, too, that if I dragged the kids back to Yucca Valley, they would be unhappy and uncooperative just when I needed them to be helpful.

I flip-flopped through the issue: Should I try to find a house and struggle through the pregnancy and birth on my own – and with children who resented me for taking them out of what they thought of as paradise, or should I stay at the Ranch where everyone, especially Collin, wanted me and would be supportive? In that case, I could commute to work the whole time or stop working anytime I wanted to. Of course, giving up the job would cost me my insurance and I would need to apply for MediCal insurance from Riverside County. I wrestled with the decision for weeks on end, never quite making it, but not doing anything toward making the move back to Yucca Valley. Simply getting through each day and doing my best to help other downtrodden folks in my confused and sometimes queasy state seemed to be about all the former superwoman could manage. In the end, the decision to remain at Freeman's Ranch was made by my own inertia.

I watched as what was left of our meager possessions became folded into the communal belongings, feeling all the while as if my lifeline to freedom was being gnawed away by circumstances, the way rodents in our old house had once gnawed electrical cords in half. It had already been painful to watch my Maytag become the communal washer. I *had* paid dearly, $100 for it and valued that possession greatly, having had to use Laundromats until after Jimmy was born. Now all my other possessions, even the scanty and worn ones, became permanently communal, dishes, pots and pans, lamps, our little sofa, etc. How was I ever going to live independently again, to scrape up new stuff to do so? I felt helpless and bewildered in the face of all of this. Although I had never placed much value on material possessions, losing them felt like the end of any chance to renew the independent life I had begun to create. As did the belly swelling in front of me.

And that belly swelled faster and larger than with any other of my five pregnancies, which had all been incredibly easy. But

I was now thirty-four. With this pregnancy, morning (more like all day) sickness stayed around much longer. The broken ribs, cracked sternum, and tendons I'd pulled from my spine in the car accident the year before made the weight of the exploding belly a problem. An African fertility statue with a hugely prominent belly sat on a shelf in the communal family room. It had always seemed laughably exaggerated. As time went on, I began to resemble that statue, until, in the end, I managed to eclipse it.

I waddled my way through work until December, when Daryl took it upon himself to call in the police after he'd dropped off the kids from the first visit he had made in months. He told the authorities that the children were being fed drugs and had been basically neglected. Fortunately, Collin and I were both there when it happened. If the cops were expecting to confront a pack of stoned hippies, they had a surprise coming when the legendary Collin O' Donally stopped them in their tracks.

The case did get turned over to Indio social services, and a social worker I'd once worked with came out to interview us and to visit the little school in session. It was a no-brainer. He said he'd like to recommend our school for other children in the area. Daryl apologized, but his action told me I needed to stay close to the place to guard my kids. I gave notice at work.

It helped some that my supervisor said I could return whenever I felt able to, that my rehiring would be automatic. I could have taken a leave, but then I wouldn't have been given the $800 plus in retirement money I'd put in, and I needed it badly. My paychecks had always gone into the communal "kitty" but I told 'the family' nothing about the retirement money. Who knew when it might come in handy?

I also signed up to substitute teach in the local schools, which brought in a little money and got me out of the commune occasionally. But most of my time I put into the School of the Dunes. It was nearing Christmas, so Collin and I and the children went caroling at local rest homes. He lined up radio interviews, too, and got a feature placed in the local paper, effectively generating good publicity for the little school and the Ranch itself. Collin had a gorgeous voice, and the children loved singing for the public. My own "can't carry a tune in a bucket" voice was a different matter. I sang softly with the rest, and no one seemed to notice.

Quitting work allowed me to be more creative with the school's curriculum. Collin and I took the children on field trips to other alternative schools. We visited local Indian tribes, studied their history and mythology. The children wrote papers about it. They learned to prepare acorns and mesquite to make flour and bread. We even put on a play where the children acted out some of the mythological stories, and Collin invited the public and officials to the play followed up by a barbeque. Those were good things and they were good for everyone – although for some of us, they were a lot more work than for others.

Just before Christmas, and a month before my supposed due date, I helped deliver Madge's baby, a large infant that weighed 8 pounds, 10 ounces on our scale. Madge delivered the baby standing up. I can still feel the wonder of guiding that beautiful creature out from between her legs and holding it up for all to see. Greg cut the cord while Cathy squeegeed the mucus from its nose. Then I wiped the bloody fluids from its skin, and handed it to Madge as the children and the rest of the family watched. No one knew exactly who the father was, and it remained a subject of discussion and argument for some time among three of the men who each claimed paternity. "Just look at the size of those balls," Dill said when he saw the child. "He has to be mine." Other evidence pointed elsewhere, and several months down the line someone else was finally awarded the honor.

There were, of course, other things going on that weren't so good. One of those other things was the BBC, or Bovine

Butchering Committee, a plot hatched in a family meeting to rustle a steer from a nearby ranch that New Year's Eve. A ranch owned by a large corporation, mind you. That meant our bellies would be full of protein for the entire winter, the rationale went, and we would be fed straight from the corporate coffers, thus subverting the oppressors. I seemed to be the only one at Freeman Ranch who wasn't at all enthusiastic. To me the idea seemed a lot more like 'acting out' than anarchism. Of course, my own anarchism and sense of social ethics were called into question.

"You're still bound by the same rules that keep the people under the thumb of the oppressor," Dill said. "That keep the rich, rich, and the poor, poor."

"You think some giant corporation that has already bought out all the real ranchers has a right to those steers," Greg said. "Just because the law says so. The poor go hungry because they can't afford meat and have no way to raise beef themselves."

"And you think you're making some kind of point by stealing that meat – and putting us all in jeopardy to do it?" I said. "Maybe if you were actually giving the meat to the poor, I would agree."

"We are the poor," Madge, a vegetarian, said, little Roy nursing at her bared breast as she spoke.

"Oh, right," I said. "I forgot. Just because we have pigs and chickens and goats and a big garden and don't even have to pay rent here. What *was* I thinking?"

"This is going to happen," said Collin, my paragon and paramour. "You might as well get used to it." He looked at me without out a smidgeon of sympathy or understanding. His face conveyed a blank coldness that chilled me. He'd never given me such a look before. It was the first of many to come, and later, that look would become as familiar as his very face. In the end, it actually became his face.

After Collin's pronouncement, the group shrugged me off and went back to plotting their silly – and dangerous –

subversive act. New Year's Eve was chosen as the target date so that the rifle shot would ring out at the stroke of midnight, blending into the rest of midnight cacophony. The spot chosen to do the deed would be a good mile away from the house where the caretaker lived. The steer murderer was to be left off with the rifle shortly before midnight, and just after midnight, after being signaled by bursts from the flashlight, the commune pickup would come back armed with hacksaws, cleavers, and butcher knives and make short and light work of the dead steer. Then the steer parts would be quickly carted to the pickup and brought back to Freeman Ranch. Books on butchering were to be studied in the meantime. I sat there hoping this harebrained scheme would fade into oblivion like so many other wild ideas I'd seen disappear. This, however, was not to be the case.

And guess who was chosen to be the shooter? Not me; I was excused because of my belly and waddle. As if I would have done it anyway. But I had given Collin some target practice while we were up at the homestead. So the group, in their wisdom, decided on Collin as their marksman. If Collin went to jail, I argued, who would be there to protect the rest of the rustlers? Of course, I didn't prevail here either. The whole project would have been hilarious if it were a TV show. But it was far too real, and I cringed to think about what might happen. And I knew one thing for certain about communal life by then: anything that happened to any one person, affected us all. Especially if it happened to the father of my baby.

If I had to choose a theme for the story of the BBC caper, it might be something like "The best-laid plans of mice and men often go awry," an Englished-up version of a line from Robert Burns' poem, "To a Mouse." The line wouldn't be quite accurate, though, since I wouldn't call the half-baked plan Freeman Ranch members laid out anywhere near 'best laid.' The mice part I can live with.

The first curve the Universe threw to send the Freeman gang scheme awry was the rare arctic storm that blew in to paint the mountains around the desert valley white and generally ice up the cactus around us on the valley floor. The storm itself was gone by New Year 's Eve evening, but it left behind extremely frigid air for the no-moon night sky, which seemed frozen solid with stars so cold they couldn't even twinkle. Naturally, being desert dwellers, none of the BBC gang had more than a light jacket around.

The second curve occurred when the gang was getting in the pickup, and Collin's hand got slammed in the door when so many of them crowded into the cab to keep from riding in the freezing truck bed. It wasn't a horrible injury, didn't quite break the skin. But it did put his hand out of commission enough so that Dill took over as the steer shooter. The gang of rustlers now reasoned that since steers were such large targets, practically anyone could hit one.

It was pitch black, Collin said later, when they let Dill out with the rifle a few minutes before midnight, so dark that the gang could only locate the cattle by the sounds of their lowing in the distance. Once in the corral, Dill had trouble finding the exact location of all that mooing, though. The steers were somewhere close by, as he could tell that much from the sounds and smells, but the darkness was so opaque that he had no idea where he was as he bumbled along among clumps of gooey cow plops. The flashlight he'd brought gave off nothing but a pale yellow-orange glow that stuttered off and on, then quit. So much for preparation. Meanwhile, he said his hands became numb from the cold. He could barely hold onto the rifle, took turns keeping one hand warm at a time down in his crotch. With his other hand, he held onto the rifle as he searched for the elusive bovines. Finally, he stumbled onto one. Literally. Smack against its side.

He said he wondered briefly how to tell the head end from the tail end in order to shoot the thing, but only very briefly because the steer took off so fast it knocked the rifle from his half-frozen hand – and because he'd taken off the safety in the interest of speedily dispatching an animal, the rifle went off. And so did fireworks and other rifles being fired around the valley. At least the timing worked.

At sound of the explosions, steers went running every which way, tromping on by him. He went running, too, trying to find some direction they weren't going. Twice he got knocked down in the manure – once by smacking into a running steer, another time by what he thought was a steer butt bumping into him – but he managed to spring up and keep going. He said he knew steers had horns and hooves, and those were parts of them he had to stay away from as he tore through the obstacle course of cattle.

Of course, by this time, Dill said he had no clue where the fence was, and after he'd bumbled around blindly for a while, thinking only to get as far as he could from any sound of the herd, he pulled the flashlight from his jacket pocket and flicked the on switch a couple times. The pale yellow light blinked on and off. He could have found the fence better with a match, he said.

Luckily, that little glimmer of flashlight was enough to bring the rest of the gang to his aid. They had heard the awaited shot and had been waiting for his signal, driving slowly up and down the empty road without headlights. Anyway, they somehow glimpsed that pale glimmer of yellow and called out to Dill – who was still some distance from the fence, but close enough to hear them as they got out of the truck and ran toward him carrying cleavers and saws and garbage bags for the butchering of the non-existent dead steer.

Meanwhile, back at Freemen Ranch, I was having my own problems. Somewhere around midnight, my hands shaking with worry over what might be happening to our committee of rustlers out in the cold dark, I was making a fresh pot of cowboy coffee on the stove. The gang would be cold when they returned, and I knew there would be work to do if they actually returned with the beef. But, somehow, between my natural clumsiness, the awkwardness of my swollen belly, and uncoordinated shaking hands, I managed to knock the pot of scalding water onto that huge bulge of belly in front of me. Happy New Year.

It would have been worse if I'd been naked, but the thin smock I wore, actually a tent-dress thing I'd made out of one of those hippie-favorite cotton tapestries from India found today in head shops, didn't offer much of a shield either. My belly turned bright red and blisters began bubbling up all over the top of the mound. I tossed cubes of ice into a plastic bread bag and held it to my stinging skin as I paced the floor, out of worry and considerable pain. My relationship to physical pain had always been, as with emotional pain, to ignore it if possible; this time it didn't work.

By the time I saw the truck's headlights wending through the rows of crucifixes, I was half out of my mind with pain and worry – and with renewed anger at the juvenile escapade. Once it became clear that the Bovine Butchering Committee had failed miserably at their task, I was both relieved and further infuriated – especially when I learned that the rifle had been left somewhere in that dark cattle pen. I saw days ahead worrying over the possibility of cops showing to arrest someone for attempted cattle rustling – Dill's prints were on file from old arrests at protests, peace marches and whatnots. Others members' prints too, most likely.

The other thing that happened that night was that after I expressed my opinion about the matter again privately in bed, Collin and I got into a cover-tugging match that ended up with the plastic bag of ice getting scattered all over our bedding, and Collin walking out to sleep in the living room. And me glad of it.

Maybe my newly awakened nesting instincts were making me more sensitive to sixties-style irresponsibility, but over the recent months Collin and I had clashed more than once over issues of his irresponsibility (in my view) in going along with stupid communal decisions that I believed ranged from unhealthy and destructive to just plain dangerous. I had lost every battle. One of these battles – a big one – involved a twenty-five-year old commune member sleeping with a barely-teen who was the daughter of one of the other new members. The girl was insisting she was fully an adult and had convinced her father of it. The rationale for such a thing was the family claim that there was no such thing as children; they were merely little people and it was proper to treat them so – a Freeman philosophy that was hauled out for rationalization, it seemed to me, whenever it was needed.

This same female "little person" had also been allowed to eat a half-ounce of hashish on her fourteenth birthday, which had resulted in another of my losing battles. I admit that this girl was extremely precocious and smart and headstrong enough to survive almost anything and thrive from it. But she was, according to any rational person such as myself, a child. This episode also cast severe doubts on the possibilities concerning my own smart and headstrong children – although the "family" assured me that anything I didn't go along with wouldn't happen. But I was coming to doubt that as well – and to doubt Collin to boot. I'd begun to wipe the fools' gold dust from my eyes.

I can't say that I fully applied this growing clarity of vision regarding Collin's and other commune members' irresponsibility to my own behavior. Even after all the psychologists I had read, I was still looking for the "answers" out there trapped fully in my own "Shadow," as Jung might have said. And the more we fail to acknowledge the 'shadow' that we cast, i.e. the darker unconscious aspects of ourselves, the more those aspects tend to dominate our behavior. As blind as I was to it then, it's easy for me to see now that my growing freedom from the mythology of Freemans' Ranch only served to send me back into my *own* mythology as the fearless rattlesnake killer. I was desperate to get my macha back. This time, however, my macha didn't involve killing rattlers but deer.

By mid-January my due date was fast approaching. Already I was far huger than I'd ever been with any of my other pregnancies. The doctor said he'd give me another week and then induce labor. What? I'd always spit out babies as easily as eating pie, and my last labor had been less than an hour. Of course, I'd been twenty-three then, not thirty-four. Still, I wasn't about to let the doctor take control over *my* body. I'd find a way to get things started on my own.

My fifth child had been accidentally 'induced' eleven years ago by sliding downhill in a cardboard box after a huge snowstorm. I'd barely gotten to the hospital in time. Well, there was no snow in Indio, and even the surrounding mountains were barren of snow this year, except for a few patches left over from that pre New Year's Eve storm. But I thought of another way that just might work – and one that would fully restore my macha superwoman identity at the same time.

My idea was that Collin and I should go deer hunting near the old homestead in Pipes Canyon, and Collin went along with it. Climbing around those mountains after deer would be sure to get my labor initiated – and we might just bring back meat for the winter. A scheme as lame-brained as the BBC, you might think, but at least it wasn't illegal. Well, actually it was – but not in my eyes, anyway. My family had never heeded rules or fees imposed by outsider game wardens – these were *our* mountains and, hence, *our* animals, and no one could tell us homesteaders any different. Besides, it had only been a couple weeks since deer season ended. That was my reasoning at the time, and the trip seemed just short of brilliant to me. I realize now I should have had my Phi Beta Kappa membership revoked – if I'd ever deserved it in the first place. Of course, academic ability and lifesmarts are entirely different matters.

I must have been quite a sight when we took off up the mountain at dawn's light after spending the night in the homestead cabin. Because my belly was so enormous and heavy, I'd secured it with a tablecloth that Collin tied behind my back. Though the temperature must have been close to zero at 6000 feet, I wore my jacket unzipped – since no jacket on the planet would have zipped up around that enormous belly. Since it was winter, I did wear shoes.

We followed an old game trail up the mountain to the deer beds. My belly made climbing difficult, but the excitement drew me on. I was on home ground. The energy of the place filled my belly with helium and helped to boost me over those steep and rugged desert mountains. At least for the first few hours we hiked. Those sparsely vegetated desert mountains weren't exactly swarming with mule deer, and after a while the helium began to leak out.

Then I spotted fresh track. That gave us another burst of energy, took us even deeper into the wild. Finally, we came over a ridge and spotted a young buck in the distance. Collin took a shot before I could stop him – we were too far away to hit the animal with my old .22, the only rifle we had around. The deer ran up and over another higher, steeper mountain, and our chance of winter meat vanished over that ridge with him.

Now entirely deflated, I looked up at the sky, then down at the lengthening shadows. The sun was getting ready to slide down behind the mountain in front of us, and here we were, sans deer, sans labor, and with what now seemed like the Himalayas between us and our car. By this time, my legs weighed fifty pounds each. Yet they felt like matchsticks as I trudged up and down the steep peaks toward home with my whale of a belly .

Looking back now, I wonder who those two people were – especially the one playing me. What if my labor had started a few mountains back? Had Collin been prepared to deliver the baby, or was I planning to stop long enough to push it out along the trail, then carry it and half of the deer we didn't get back with me? Or maybe, as superwoman, I could have just flown us all out of there.

Is it plausible that perhaps something in me already knew what the doctor would tell me the following week, after he finally ex-rayed my belly. Did my body already know that there was not one baby inside me, but two?

When I heard that news a few days later, I literally fell straight back into the arms of the nurse behind me. I had just been thrown the biggest surprise of my life. The doctor added that, besides there definitely being two babies, there could be yet another one hiding behind them. That was what had tipped me backwards. The doctor also said that he was worried about how big I was – my five foot, small-frame body was getting almost as wide as it was tall. He said he might have to take the babies by cesarean section "down the road." Indeed, it was hard to imagine that the already Guinness-World-Record-sized watermelon in front of me was not yet through growing and wouldn't be for two more months.

I hadn't expected a litter. Hearing that it was not *a* baby but two bab*ies*, and possibly three (which thank the Universe it wasn't), stunned me deeply. None of my children had been conceived without escaping through some form of birth control – but I had trusted that IUD. After the latest news, I wondered if the device might just have split an egg in half or into pieces. Impossible, of course, but no one in our family had ever had twins. Neither, said Collin, had anyone in his family. Collin, by the way, was thrilled. He did everything but beat his chest. Oh, wait, I remember he did that, too.

I must have gone through the remainder of the pregnancy in that same stunned state, since the memory of those weeks is mostly a blur. I know I continued to teach at our School of the Dunes and occasionally substituted in the public school, wrote dark poetry while Collin painted his watercolors, cooked meals, washed clothes, etc. I do remember vividly, though, that inside me, the babies were constantly at war, fighting for the space that each one thought should be its alone. It's a wonder they weren't born bruised and battered from all the kicking that went on. I was concerned for those babies, was sorry that each one would not have its life and birth all to itself, worried that they were being born without the space each of them deserved as individual beings. As for my own self, I felt as if the Universe had kicked the last spark of superwoman out my system and this time stuffed my entire inside with Kryptonite in a living taxidermy of sorts.

One other thing happened, too, that day, something that would eventually be my lifeline back to the world. I came home to find a letter from the university saying I had been awarded a graduate fellowship for the following school year. At the time, the award seemed like the darkest of jokes. Here I was, living in a commune about to give birth to twins (at least), and now came a ticket to start graduate school with babies who would be only four or five months old. Now let's see: I'd be going to school while managing a ten-year-old and four others aged between twelve and seventeen, along with two or more new infants. I don't think so. So what did I do? The only thing I could do, what I always did: I disregarded reality, signed the acceptance letter and sent it back.

Chapter fifteen
Afterbirth

Originally, the idea had been for me to have an unattended home birth at Freeman's Ranch, but when the *baby* became the *babies*, I insisted on having a hospital birth with a doctor present. This of course put my credentials as a "natural woman" further into question. For family members, it also further indicated my disdain for the mystique of the afterbirth. There had been huge arguments over Madge's afterbirth, known to most of us as the placenta. Some thought this powerful object needed to be taken far away and buried, so that Marge's child would not become too much of a mama's boy. Others thought it should be buried outside in the yard to root the child to that place. I don't remember what the argument was that, in the end, made the family boil up the placenta and have members eat it – which I didn't do, nor did I allow my children to. I think it had something to do with protein and with making the new "little person" a part of everyone. Giving birth in a hospital would ensure that my own placenta wouldn't become the object of another hippy-dippy controversy.

Anyway, I waddled around like an elephant on two hind legs until early March. This was like no pregnancy I had ever experienced. Simply getting from place to place was a major chore, but staying put was almost as hard, as was sleeping or sitting. My doctor was genuinely worried that waiting any longer would do harm to both myself and the babies, and living in my out-of-proportion body told me he was right. He pleaded with me to induce. By mid-March, I agreed to the inducement shots and stayed several hours in the hospital, waiting for the medication to have its affect. Collin stayed with me, eager for the birth. Yet, after several hours of unproductive contractions, I decided this was not something I should be doing. Collin agreed, and we got out of there. When we came back at the end of the month, I was in labor for real.

But this labor was certainly nothing like the easy labors I'd experienced before. It lasted for several long and extremely painful hours until the end, when the two babies shot out so fast they almost knocked the nurses over. One was almost six pounds, the other not quite four pounds. I found it hard to believe I had swelled up to such gigantic proportions because of creatures that small. And there were only two, thank the Universe. Whew! Collin had never given up hoping for three.

The following day, I was allowed to leave the hospital, but with only the almost six-pound, John. The other infant, Michael, the pediatrician said, had to remain until he gained a few more ounces, even though he was perfectly healthy and not really premature. I didn't at all like leaving my child in that sterile and impersonal place, so later that evening when I came back to breastfeed little Michael, I brought his clothes and dressed him. Then I informed the nurse I was taking him with me. Collin had come with me to furnish the legal justification. As we expected, hospital personnel freaked out and called the pediatrician, the only person who could legally hinder us by getting Child Protective Services involved. She asked to speak with me by phone and tried to tell me that taking Michael home would be harming him. I reminded her that I'd had considerable experience with babies, and that the best thing for this underweight but otherwise healthy baby was to have the kind of attention only I would be able to give him – at home. In the end, she said she was very angry about what we were doing but that she wouldn't call CPS. She made me promise I would call her any hour of the day if I sensed any problem at all.

We had won. Now all we had to do was survive taking care of two underweight newborns under communal conditions. Michael needed to be fed every hour and a half, while John could go a whole three hours. To keep the constant stream of communal noises from waking them, we filled the air of our room with a constant stream of our own – music from Collin's Classical collection. '78s stayed stacked up like vinyl pancakes on Collin's record player at all times. Sleep became a thing of the past. For me certainly, but also for Collin, who hung in like I'd never seen Daryl do, and for several weeks we dragged hungry, crying babies from the basinet to the bed, the two of us wandering around for weeks in a mutual fog like some kind of zombie parents. The babies, however, were definitely not zombies and seemed to be awake all of the time.

At the height of our passionate first three weeks, Collin and I had rarely left the room together except for trips out to the dunes after everyone else was asleep. Other times, one of us would go out to the bathroom or to bring back food. Now we were locked in a similar cycle, minus the passionate sex and nights on the dunes. After a few days I was able to stay out of the room longer and make formula to supplement the breast milk that didn't go far enough for these perpetually awake eating machines, who seemed to be doing an excellent job of gaining the weight they needed. We did have one close call with Michael, when his rubber pants (the things we used to put over diapers to keep infants dry in those days of ancient history) leaked in the night and I discovered his little body all wet and way too cold. He hadn't even cried. After I changed him and wrapped him in a thin blanket, I wrapped that in a heating pad and heated him back up to normal.

We allowed the babies' brothers and sisters as well as communal family members to come into the room and hold the babies, but it was three weeks before I felt the twins were strong enough to visit the family room, exposing them to massive communal germs, including germs from the perpetual collection of visitors. This "attitude" of mine more than annoyed the "family." According to them, the twins were not at all tiny newborns with still fragile immune systems that needed to be gradually exposed to various bacteria. But I was trying to warp them into being just that when they were really tiny people fully formed and fit to be exposed to every germ lurking in the universe.

My "attitude" that I was the rightful authority on their well-being came into question more and more often as the months went by. The new babies were regarded as 'communal children.' But that was strictly theoretical, having nothing to do with being responsible for taking care of them night and day. It did apply to what kind of milk, food, behaviors, etc, were good for the babies. If the family had its way, decisions about their care would have been a matter for endless family meetings. I would have none of it, of course. I found the idea outrageous that a group of mostly twenties males, and three or four females, only one of whom had any child-raising experience, could possibly think they knew better than I did what was good for my babies.

Collin, for the most part, ignored the family's interference, although he didn't jump in and support me either. Once the babies began sleeping at least most of the night, he pretty much went back to his old routines and left the rest to me. He did watch and play with his babies often and loved doing it. But we began to have frequent fights ourselves over baby-raising. As the weeks went on, we clashed more and more often: I remember coming home from a trip to the grocery store and finding him holding a crying baby while watching a football game. I could smell the dirty diaper the minute I came into the room, but when I pointed out to him that this was why the baby was screaming his lungs out, he told me it was none of my business and that he would take care of his babies the way he saw fit. It took a while before he would even give up the child so that I could change him and put salve on the painful red skin caused by wearing that dirty diaper so long.

Collin changed over the next few months. Fairly dramatically. Sometimes he seemed to be staring past me as we talked, as if I were invisible. He stayed stoned much of the time. When I tried to talk with him about this change, he came up with two custom-made epithets to club me with: "Stupid Yucca Valley Bitch" and "Sour-faced bitch," the latter used if he saw so much of a tear spring into my eyes. And if he didn't like whatever spontaneous expression appeared on my face in response to something he'd said or done, he would mock the expression dramatically, as well as sarcastically repeat any words I might manage to mutter. Collin became someone I no longer knew.

I don't know if my decision to accept the fellowship and go back to the university that fall had anything to do with all of this. I doubt it. Certainly, the family was happy about the money that would go into communal coffers. I suspect they were also glad I'd be out of the place two days a week. Yet each time I left the house for the university, it was with trepidation. I couldn't fully trust Collin, even with the help of my now three teenagers to take care of the two five-month-olds, not even with a list of written instructions (they would all just ignore them).

It didn't take long before I realized that I had never taken on anything so difficult as trying to attend graduate school under such conditions. On the days I didn't make the ninety-six mile, all-day trip in for classes, not only did I have a heavy load of homework to do as I cared for the infants, but I remained the mainstay for the alternative school that my other children needed. Most of the others had stopped making contributions once the newness wore off. I was finding zero time for research and paper writing, and graduate work is 80% homework.

Sometime during those first weeks of school, John developed bronchitis so bad that the pediatrician admitted him to the hospital, where he stayed for two days with me at his crib side day and night, doing as much homework as I could. Collin visited but didn't see the need to stay nights with his child and spell me so I could get some sleep. At one point, I needed to get away for an hour to shower but when I called Collin to see if he'd come take my place, I was told he was out playing golf for the afternoon. I felt the last speck of trust in him go out of me.

Yet beyond all the family responsibilities and lack of support that made my first graduate semester such a nightmare, something more seriously personal about graduate work concerned me. During my time as an undergraduate, joyous insights went off like fire rockets whenever I read the authors I was studying. Thematic connections between the authors' works would crisscross my brain, making writing a paper a pleasurable fulfillment. All I needed to do to write papers was to scan through enough critics' work to back up my own ideas. But five weeks into graduate school, I was reading critics almost entirely and assessing their insights on each assigned author's work – which was more painful than fun. And instead of professors being thoroughly impressed when I turned in a paper, I would hear things like, "This isn't graduate work," or "You need to make your connections stronger," or "Your idea here could be publishable, but you'll have to do more thorough research." Even though I knew I wasn't the only new graduate student hearing these things, I seriously considered the possibility that the accident had permanently diminished my brain capacity.

The fights Collin and I had reached new levels of ugliness. Whenever I tried to discuss any given issue we were having, Collin would refuse to participate, and after not much more on his part than highly refined – and remember this was one brilliant and extremely articulate man – name-calling and mockery, he would stop speaking to me completely. Of course, I wouldn't let him off without first trying to harangue him into being a human being – which never worked. The more I tried to rationally discuss the matter and ask him to tell me what he was angry about, the meaner he would become – and for longer periods. Sometimes the pain of it would lead to my crying, which only made things worse yet. Then one day, when I wouldn't give up my pursuit to make him understand, he got up from his chair and calmly ripped up every single one of the beautiful watercolors he had painted. Paintings I loved. When I tried to get him to stop, he shoved me away and went on with his methodical ripping and tearing of all the beauty he had created. It was that icy calmness that finally backed me off. I felt chilled to the bone with the utter self-destruction of his act. It seemed to have torn apart whatever love I still felt for him.

I walked around stunned for a few days. I finally got it – finally understood that no matter what I did things would never go back to the loving relationship we'd had in the beginning. When I approached him in tears, saying I thought there was nothing left for me to do but leave, all he said was, "Don't let the door hit your ass on the way out." No surprise, but that was not the response I had hoped for.

The final incident, though, that clenched my leaving the commune took place the following week and had minimally little to do with Collin. I'd come home from the university to find the yard cluttered with ragtag, tangled-haired men and women dressed in filthy burlap sacks that were tied at the waist with rope. Those ropes also hosted on most of the males, homemade scabbards that held enormous hunting knifes. I found the strange visitors lurking in other places, too, as I went on a mad search for my children. Gunny-sack people lounged around the porch, the family room, the kitchen. I heard a conversation snippet as I flew past: "Oh, that's nothing. The last time *I* had hepatitis....."

I was relieved to discover my three daughters huddling in Collin's and my room with the babies. The scene was even too weird for them. Jimmy had left to play with the neighbor kids across the dunes. The girls said the entire family was out back having a meeting about what to do with the weird group – who were apparently disciples of one of the members who called himself John the Baptist. Dill had found them on the side of the road and brought them all home on a lark. Now they didn't know how to get rid of them.

When I headed out to find the family, I came across John the Baptist himself. He had climbed onto a kitchen chair and was preaching the gospel to empty air. His eyes were wild and his dark matted hair stood out around his head. His was the face of pure insanity. The others couldn't have been far behind him, I surmised. Why else would they be following him? I'd had enough experience with psychotic people from my social work case load, let alone with Daryl and Mother, to trust my instincts – and those instincts said there was even more here than simple psychosis here. There was a real danger.

Apparently, the family had come to this conclusion, too, before I arrived, which is why they were out back trying to figure out what to do now. They were afraid to simply ask the knife-bearing group to leave. Everyone agreed that Dill was responsible – but he was also too small to handle it by himself. In the end, it was decided that Dill, along with three other "big guys" would escort the group out with pickups and drop them off in Joshua Tree National Monument (now a National Park), where they could camp for free. Many sandwiches, some cash, and gallons of water would be sent with them.

Although the family in the end did attend to this particular situation responsibly, I wasn't at all certain that other such situations wouldn't occur in the future. And what would stop these people from coming back? An assortment of odd people wandered in and out of Freeman's Ranch all the time. (The perception of danger from this particular group was validated the following summer when John the Baptist made headlines after the police shot him for waving a gun around as he preached in Yosemite National Park. By then he'd gone full-bore and was shouting that he was Jesus Christ himself.)

I'd never cottoned to the surrender of control over my life required to live at Freeman's ranch, but this issue was far more serious. I finally realized that the place exposed my children to more danger than I'd been willing to look at, especially now that I wasn't around as much to look out for them myself. I was already suspicious about family teenage boys sharing their pot and who knew what else with my girls. That concern and the complete deterioration of my relationship with Collin made me realize I had to get us out of there. Now.

But how? Almost everything we'd brought had been swallowed up into communal sharing. And I knew Kim and Linda would be dead set against leaving. Renee too. She was nearing eighteen, and her new boyfriend lived near Freeman's Ranch. Already the two of them were talking about marriage. And I was in the middle of the first term of graduate school. Leaving was not going to be easy.

I called on my friend Diana for help. Diana knew of a three-bedroom house for rent and said she could round up some mattresses and other furniture that her clients had stored in garages. The timing was good, as another fellowship check had just arrived that day – and I still had some of my stash of social work retirement money left. Dishes pots and pans I could get at thrift stores. The rest we'd work out. When I was ready to make my move, I told Collin I was leaving with my children, for the good of us all.

"Who the fuck do you think you are?" he shouted when he saw I was serious. "Breaking up a family like this." His stood there, his face shading toward purple, fists clenched, his body tensed like a cougar about to pounce.

For a moment I wondered if I might be in physical danger from this former boxer. More than once, I had seen him wrestle unruly intruders a foot taller than himself to the ground in about two seconds. I realized that no matter what he'd said before, he just couldn't believe I'd actually leave. I couldn't believe he doubted it – or that he cared. Our "conversations" had become not much more than an occasional snarl at each other.

I held back the words on my tongue, which were *Oh, go fuck a gunnysack,* and instead decided on the more rational reaction. "Breaking up what family? I'm taking my family with me, that's all," I said. "As in my own children."

"They're not your children anymore. They belong to all of us."

"Fuck that. Tell that bullshit to the cops, mister attorney, when I claim the family kidnapped and brainwashed them. The law's on my side here."

His face drained of color. "You fucking bitch," he said.

"You haven't seen anything yet." I turned to leave. "Just try and stop me and see what happens."

"You're not taking my sons with you."

I turned back. "Okay, what if I *were* to leave them here. Who the hell would take care of them? All the touted 'communal parenting' just isn't happening around this place."

"That's because you never *let* it happen, bitch."

"Right! It's always my fault. I forgot. Everyone here is willing to offer advice about how to raise my babies – but no one ever wants to change a diaper or hold a baby for more than five seconds. Except for the baby's own sisters – and they resent the hell out of it. No way on earth will I leave those babies here."

I swung around and left the bedroom, yet I couldn't help but yell back, "Well, what do you know – your door didn't come near my ass." Despite my smart retort, I found it very painful to leave this man I once idolized. That confused me. I couldn't understand how I could have any feelings left for him after he'd been so despicable to me. It's easy to see now that my view of my own emotional life was vastly oversimplified. I suppose that had helped me survive – and I had never connected as deeply with anyone as I had Collin. I wasn't prepared for the grief my decision brought me.

Chapter Sixteen
The Rough Road Back

I had the kids waiting for me in the car far down the driveway – but under false pretenses. I'd told them that we were going up to spend the weekend with Diana and her children, two of whom were having birthday parties (that part was true). And we did go to Diana's house. I let them spend a night before I told them that we weren't going back to Freeman's Ranch except in a few days for more clothes and other possessions. Timmy was already in Yucca Valley, staying with his friend's family, since he had never joined us. Now he would live with us again. And I was sure that Jimmy would be excited about the move back home.

The girls sure weren't. "I hate you. You can't make us leave," Kim and Linda kept screaming at me, over and over as we drove up to the new house "We'll hitch back to the ranch. You can't stop us."

"You do that and I'll just have the cops bring you back. Put the family in jail and you in juvie for a while, maybe," I told them. I hoped like hell I could out-bluff these headstrong little witches. (How someone as passive as I was could have such daughters, I just didn't know.)

Renee just sat there with tears running down her cheeks. I knew the situation for her was more serious. If it had been the days of cell phones, she would have been on one. But it wasn't, and we didn't even have a phone of any kind in the new house yet.

For the next few months, I was the most hated mother on the planet. After a few weeks, when things calmed down, I relented some and let them spend occasional weekends at the Ranch – cautioning them that any move to remain there would mean I'd call the cops on the Freeman Ranch "family" and then everyone involved would be in trouble. Except for continuing to hate me, Kim, Linda and Jimmy adjusted fairly well, resuming old friendships and doing surprisingly well in public school again. Our little School of the Dunes had put them ahead of their classmates academically.

Renee was a different story. She moped. And moped. Then one day I came home from school and found that her boyfriend had driven up and taken her away. She would soon marry him. I didn't fight it; she was almost eighteen, and they would stay together for several years until he was killed by a drunk driver, leaving her with two young children to finish raising.

The months went by in a blur of vain attempts at homework, while running after newly mobile twins, each one with ten times more energy than any one baby should have. They went to bed late, woke up early, even when they kept me up most of the night with their ear infections. The ear infections seemed to have zero affect on their energy, though it sapped mine to the core. The more mobile the babies got, the more adventurous they became, which resulted in odd accidents happening right before my eyes before I could make it across the room to stop them. We made visits to the emergency room for stitches and burns from hot beverages they had found creative ways to reach, me dragging my books along with us, then trying to read while comforting the injured child and chasing after his ever-energetic brother.

On the two days I drove to Riverside for classes, I took John and Michael to stay with my Diana, who had become the babysitter supreme of Yucca Valley. Kim, Linda and Jimmy would go there, too, after school, to play with her children. I would return in the evening and take us all home – which was only two blocks away. Timmy was usually spending time with friends, in fact, more time with friends than he should have during his senior year. I was too preoccupied to notice. I suppose far too many other important things at home went by unnoticed in that memory blur, as I tried to understand and write papers on Alexander Bain's influence on the way composition is taught in public schools, or Percy Shelley's influence on Lord Byron's poetry. Or was it visa versa? It wasn't as if the work required in graduate school brought the same joyful insights I found in undergraduate studies. That would have given me respite. Except for a few little glimmers where I dared take risks – such as my paper about Jungian archetypes in Shelley's poetry – completing papers became pure drudgery. By this time, I had figured out just what was expected with graduate work. Yet the fear continued to haunt me that the reason school work was now so hard had to do with a brain damaged by my accident two years before. The woman who not so long ago felt she had much to give back to the universe was now desperately trying to survive the new life she had created for herself and her children.

When I look back at the me I was then, I can see how stretched to the limits I was at the time. I still hadn't fully conceded that even I had limits. I remember writing terrible poems filled with the ever-present hurt, fear and confusion I felt. If I had hoped that leaving the commune would help me reconnect with my former superwoman self, what I found in her place was some broken shell of that self, floundering and about to drown in the deep waters around her. I clung to the beauty of every sunset and flower I saw to strengthen and see me through each day. To change metaphors yet again, I was on a frayed tightrope, walking across a Grand Canyon of impossibilities. But I wouldn't let myself give in to the chasm looming below me. As I had done throughout my life before and since, I kept putting one foot in front of me as the rope bounced and swayed, kept my eyes on the distant bank, knowing that was the only way I'd reach the other side, or in this case, the end of the school year.

Meanwhile, Collin continued to visit his sons. He even contributed cash for their support, about $150 per month, that he earned from a new sign painting business he was operating out of Freeman's Ranch. I can't tell you how much all this impressed me. Daryl had never contributed a dime, despite the court order, and only visited the children occasionally – which was usually to stir up some kind of trouble. During the time I worked as a social worker, I'd seen how "normal" it was for some men to simply shrug off their responsibilities. I guess I had assumed that Collin would do something similar. And with him there was no divorce or court order. The fact that he'd started the sign painting business in order to contribute – and that he genuinely wanted to keep his relationship with the twins strong was almost a shock to me. I began to develop a grudging respect for him, one not based on self-delusion.

He made it clear, too, that seeing his sons wasn't the only reason he made the visits, and that I was welcome back in his life at the ranch whenever I was ready. We were bonded for life, he would say, by the babies and by our feelings for each other. I couldn't deny the pain of our separation, although it was still much less than the pain I had felt living with him. My feelings for Collin reached much deeper into who I'd been becoming than those for Daryl ever had. Yet, even though the charming Collin who visited us now showed no sign of being the asshole bastard I'd escaped, I knew he was in there somewhere. Besides, I had zero desire to return to communal life, and I couldn't see Collin ever leaving the community he'd formed. Time and building a new life in my old territory would be my antidotes to him. I hoped.

I did make it to the end of the school year and, in a state of hopeless bewilderment, I nevertheless signed the contract to be a teaching assistant for the following year. I hadn't a shred of the bravado I usually operated on. I couldn't believe the professors were still willing to continue to support my studies after all my flailing around in graduate work – and offering me a teaching assistantship when I had ended the semester with three incompletes. Not only would I face taking the normal load of graduate classes for the upcoming year, but add to that making up the three incompletes, teaching a freshman composition class, studying for Comprehensive Exams I'd have to take, studying for the Graduate Record Exam I'd have to take to prove my dexterity in the Spanish Language, let alone facing "The Committee" on a thesis paper I had yet to write. Reality had already kicked my butt. Now it was getting ready to grind my face into the ground

I still don't know why I signed those papers. I had no intention of continuing, at least no conscious intention. Not because I didn't want to, but because I had zero belief left that I would be able to succeed, based solidly on my experience the year before.

The decision to take the three incompletes had come with realizing what was required for successful graduate work. It would be far better for my grade-point average if I took the time to do more research and quality writing rather than turn in slipshod papers that I hadn't had enough time to work on properly. But I also knew that to complete the papers during the summer while working a job was going to be a huge challenge. And I couldn't expect any help from my daughters who had wheedled me into letting them spend much of the summer at the Ranch. Not to mention that the university library was ninety miles away in Riverside. As far as another year of grad school, I had reached the other side of the enormous chasm only to find another much larger chasm that needed to be crossed, and the tightrope under my feet was far too frayed to get me there.

I explained all this to Collin when I drove down to Freeman's Ranch to deliver Linda and Kim for their first summer stint there, which they had earned by keeping their grades up and laying off bitching at me for their two evening a week babysitting chore. I remember telling him my story as we sat out under clusters of purple wisteria, the twins running and tumbling on the grass in front of us. I used a different metaphor then, saying that I felt as if I had made it nearly to the peak of Mount Everest, but just when I was ready to tackle the final and steepest slope, I found I had two broken legs and a sprained arm. There was no way I could climb the rest of the way to the top, even if I crawled. Reality had finally set in – I had gotten through the semester, but was ready to cut my losses, forget being a grad student for next year. I figured I would finish up the incompletes I already had, then see where to go from there, which wouldn't be the university. I told him there was no way I could succeed with the extreme requirements that would be demanded for the next year and that I was ready to find a full-time job, to return to social work most likely, although the faith I'd once had in my ability to help anyone seemed to have vanished as well.

Collin must have heard me. He asked a few questions, perhaps to make sure I wasn't exaggerating, then said, "You do have to get this degree. What if I came to live with you? I could take over watching the boys. You could use all your time to study. We could even move down into student housing for the year if that would make it easier for you."

The sound of those words felt like the first drop of rainwater after a parching drought. Yet merely the thought of living with Collin again sent a bolt of fear into my gut and set off alarms in my rational self. At the same time I knew this was the only chance I had of getting that degree. So I said something like, "Well, maybe that *would* be feasible," thinking that would keep the subject open and give me some time to think this over before I talked with him again. I was shocked that he'd even consider leaving the commune that he had co-founded. I didn't think he was entirely serious but simply trying on an idea, the way I always did when making decisions. That, however, was not the way Collin operated.

After we discussed some ways our arrangement might work, Collin told me he needed to talk with some family members and he went into the house. I sat outside watching John and Michael play, mulling over the prospect. I felt surprised and grateful. But also afraid, my reservations becoming more pronounced by the minute. When Collin returned a few minutes later carrying the old suitcase he kept in his closet, I realized that he had meant to act *now*. It was a real oh-my-god moment. I'd assumed he'd gone to family members about some issue or another – not about what he'd just proposed to me. I was profoundly dumbfounded.

"Let's round up the boys then," he said. And in my stunned state I went along with it all, getting the twins into the car and driving down the driveway, as if it actually was a decision I'd been in on and wholly agreed with. Collin and I talked about making a new start of things and me getting my degree. He'd already gone the degree route, he said, then found a law career was not for him. He seemed convinced it would work differently for me. I listened and must have taken part in that conversation. But all I remember is being befuddled the whole way back to Yucca Valley – and beyond. Was I really going through with this? This had to be some kind of dream or nightmare didn't it? Collin seemed to have that effect on my life.

But was I really so passive through it all? I know at the time I felt helpless, caught in the wake of forces taking me where I wasn't at all sure I wanted to go. Or was that 'someone-smarter-than-I-am' inside me taking the reins again and manipulating the situation to guide me toward where I needed to go, despite my conscious reluctance? Well, who knows? I wouldn't put it past her.

Chapter Seventeen
Superwoman Modified

The summer Collin and I spent together on our own was a pleasant one – much to my surprise. I don't think we fought once. We enjoyed sharing parenting, became amazed as the twins developed their own sound language that they used in addition to the normal words they were quickly picking up. It turned out that they were incredibly sensitive to sound. The two of them would mouth a certain click sound that meant turn on the light, and a slightly different one for turning it off. Both 'sound words' seemed to be based on the actual sound of the light switch. They were both extremely sensitive to the nuances of sound. They especially liked the sounds of automobiles. I remember watching the two of them stand on the sofa by the window and argue vigorously by mimicking various motor noises, the issue apparently being just what kind of vehicle was about to come around the corner and into sight. For silent things and concepts, they used actual words.

Our relationship felt so harmonious that by the end of the summer, Collin and I decided to get married and move into student housing in Riverside for the coming year. With teaching and all the catch-up work I would have to do, my usual two-day-a-week ninety mile commute didn't seem feasible. So we had a lovely hippie-like ceremony in Joshua Tree National Park – Greg Butcherside had recently received a mail-order Universalist Church Minister ordination – then a tailgate party afterward for family and friends, both straight and very much otherwise – straight in those days meaning conventional and non-dope using. Pictures show the two of us radiant and in love against the picturesque rock formations. They show nothing of the ambivalence that kept me nauseated for the next two days. I knew I couldn't be pregnant since I'd had a tubal ligation after the twins were born.

Once classes started, I set up a schedule that had me

studying sixteen to eighteen hours a day. I would spend an hour a day studying Spanish, two hours memorizing poems and poets for the Comprehensive Exam, several hours working on the incompletes, more hours marking papers and preparing for the classes I taught, many other hours studying and writing papers for the classes I was taking, and the rest on my thesis paper. I did most of my work in the bedroom at home, except when I was attending classes or teaching them. While working at home, I could take breaks and play with the twins, ask the girls and Jimmy about how school was going, and say hi to Collin. I continued doing most of the cooking and laundry in between studying, as well. Chores brought relief. Collin became the dishwasher and general picker-upper. And he painted signs for extra cash. I have a newspaper clipping showing our clothesline hung with painted signs and Linda, who was now lovely and fifteen, hanging up another of his signs to dry.

During the spring and final quarter before graduation, once I had made up my incompletes, I was able to fill up those several hours a week by adding job hunting to my schedule. It was a fruitless effort for the most part, since a recession had hit, and Proposition 13 in California had changed the community college teaching landscape (and what else could an English major with an M.A. do but teach at community colleges?). I think only three community college positions in English composition were open in the entire state that year. I did hear of a job prospect in Salinas, though. The position was for a Spanish speaker, and involved teaching the English language, along with confident body language to immigrants so they could deal with La Migra and the rest of American culture. I set up a week-long working-in-the-field interview to begin the week after graduation.

Whatever had happened to the feeling of being free and fully alive I once had? I was far too busy to ask. Too mired in studies and family even to notice it was gone.

Meanwhile, things were getting less rosy between Collin

and me, though I can't for the life of me remember what the specific issues were. I never knew which Collin I'd be dealing with – the tender loving Collin, or the ass whose response to my complaints was to ignore them and me and anything I said – which drove me up the wall – or the one who would mock my expression and whatever I said, which also drove me up the wall and turned me into a screaming, crying witch at times. I wondered if I'd married my mother, psychologically speaking, but a more potent version. Sometimes I even wondered if I was becoming her – except that she had always been the one with power in her relationship with my dad. I seemed to have none.

I realize I couldn't have been as innocent as I felt in all this, though I thought so at the time. I must have been quite stressed from working non-stop for so many months. Collin had more sense than to work himself to a frazzle, and by the second quarter he had the twins in a collective pre-school four hours a day, was golfing twice a week, and even playing soccer occasionally. I suspect much of his freedom was bought at the expense of my picking up slack and that's what the issues were about.

It wasn't so much our clash of ideas and issues that got to me, but the methods Collin used to fight. For me, the battles were separate from how we felt and treated each other; for Collin, the way we treated each other (and therefore *appeared* to feel about each other) was a legitimate weapon of battle. And he was skilled at battle – first as a fabled street scrapper in Dublin, then as a champion boxer, and finally as a legendary courtroom professional, who juggled legal arguments as easily as saying hello. As far as I was concerned, the argumentative strategies he used to cut me to ribbons were highly illegal on an emotional level, something you just don't do to someone you love.

Still, between rounds, he came through for me with bouts of sweetness. I remember his having constructed a mortarboard cap for me out of poster cardboard the day I was given the all-clear for the graduation ceremony that I didn't stay around for.

Instead, I put on the cardboard cap, and we got into our already packed VW bus and headed out for Salinas and my working job interview, which was to start the next day. Linda and Jimmy came with us. Kim went back to the ranch and the boyfriend she'd found there.

The outcome of this trying year sounds much simpler than it was at the time. The truth is, my brain was totally fried by the time that horrific school year was over. I had ended my extensive job hunt with at least the prospect of a job, graded my students, completed my incompletes, passed all my own classes, as well as passed the Spanish Record Exam, the Comprehensive Exam, and the Thesis Committee Exam with the highest scores of any of my fellow students – yet afterward I was not able to speak a coherent sentence in English. I remember how during the next two weeks, I continually left out words and phrases from my sentences, conflated concepts and objects, even called things by homonymic or synonymic misnomers. For some strange reason, I stayed more articulate in Spanish. And it was a good thing since I spent the next week working in the barrios as a part of my interview. I got the job, too, and was to begin working in another month.

With the prospect of soon having a decent income and interesting job that combined teaching and social work, I felt deliriously happy and ready to enjoy some summer camping with what was left of my family. We had saved up summer funds and stashed a ton of food.

I was probably delirious to begin with, and more relieved that it was over than I was happy. I was thrilled to be freed from the academic world. The department offered me continued fellowship support for Ph. D. work, but this time I declined without hesitation. Maybe if they'd signaled approval of the topic I'd proposed – Jungian archetypes in Hopi and Navajo oral stories – rather than asking, "But who could possibly be on your committee?" I might have considered it. But I doubt it. I had no desire to remain in academia. With the shiny new power tool of a master's degree, I was eager to begin my adventures in the Real World. Besides, I had discovered how much I enjoyed teaching.

I can't say I crossed the academic finish line feeling free and fully alive the way I had in the past, though. I felt more like I'd been spit out of a meat grinder. But I had shown myself that I was still able to pull off what was needed against considerable odds, despite my somewhat damaged but still tender brain. At the same time, I had a better sense of my own limits after the fiasco of my first year of studies. My superwoman self had been modified considerably.

I also knew I couldn't have accomplished this feat without Collin's help, and I felt a dangerous gratitude toward him. Dangerous because I didn't want to need this man who affected me so powerfully, yet who seemed willing to go far out of bounds to keep me at bay. "You're Genghis Khan," he said more than once. "You'd just run right over me with hobnail boots if I let you." That he viewed me in such a manner was incomprehensible to me at that time when I felt so powerless in our relationship. I didn't feel powerless about affecting things in the bigger world around us, though. I knew well my strengths there. I wonder now if that very confidence is what made him wary of me. A dear friend of mine claims that at the heart of every couple's relationship is a struggle for power – if not power over the other for control-sake, then power over the other to have control over one's own life – since everything either partner does has an effect on the other's life. I do have to admit that I was determined not to let him or anyone else stop me from doing what I thought was best for my own life and for the family's economic well-being. I had spent too many years struggling to survive with very little resources.

Yet things were still good enough between us that I was willing to continue trying to be 'we.' Collin said *he* was in it for the long run. I remember how we toasted our relationship on our first anniversary: "To the death," we said, and clinked our wine glasses just shy of breaking.

In my memory of that anniversary dinner – we'd left the twins with the girls and gone out to a Chinese restaurant – it was me that came up with that ambiguous toast. But it could just as easily have been Collin. All I knew then was that the toast seemed to encapsulate the tone of our relationship – the competition, the depth of our attachment to one another, and the inability of either of us to escape that reality. It was not a healthy toast – but it was an honest one. Our dinner had brought the usual tension. I remember how Collin insisted we should order a few dishes to share and I went along with it, reluctantly, knowing that he would eat the lion's share of each dish, that I'd get one out of four of the shrimp, etc. I think that was the night I began to separate out the portions so that wouldn't happen – which Collin didn't like at all. It was petty competitions like this that dominated much of our interactions. So, 'to the death' seemed the perfect toast for the two of us.

Chapter Eighteen
Detour

As usual, things quickly went awry, askew, amiss, or whichever other synonym for knocked-cockeyed one might think of, and I never made it to my English on Wheels job. On our way to Salinas, we'd stopped off at Freeman's Ranch for a "Leo" party to celebrate my upcoming birthday and that of several other Leos. I was the only person at that celebration, other than the children, who stayed completely sober – not a drop of alcohol or a drag of pot. Somebody had to be alert and for sure no one else was going to stay that way. Actually, this was a role I often seemed to play at the place. But I wasn't concerned. I knew that this time when the party was over, we'd be starting a new life several hundred miles away – which was party enough for me. Or so I thought.

The communal family and invited guests were partying on the grass around the lake. Barbeques were asmoke with food and most everyone took dips in the lake, some with bathing suits, some without. I had always enjoyed watching children and adults take turns swinging out on a rope from Isadora, the graceful poplar tree, and dropping down into the water. On a whim, perhaps because I had never done so before and this might be the last chance to do so before we moved north, I decided to swing out of Isadora and drop into the lake myself. Sort of as a goodbye to the place, I think now. Unfortunately, I must not have watched others closely enough, and I failed to keep my knees up, which caused me to hit my right foot and ankle on the edge of the bank just as I went into the water – which broke every single bone in that ankle, leaving my foot to flop around from side to side.

I dragged myself out of the lake and onto the dirt, then managed to get someone's attention. At first none of the fun-lovers would believe my ankle was really broken, even as I moved it from side to side to show them. "But are you *sure* it's broken?" they kept asking. No one wanted to deal with *that* bummer. I assured them it was and then directed them on how to make a chair with their arms, lift me up, then carry me to the car, and drive me to the emergency room. I so hated to leave my teenage children at that party without my supervision, and to leave them in charge of John and Michael as well. But I had absolutely no choice. I did have the presence of mind to make sure I took my purse with me; it contained all we'd saved to start our new life.

I remember being certain that amputation was imminent. I had to wait several hours for the orthopedic surgeon to drive back from Los Angeles to the desert to treat me. He had prescribed pain medication for me by phone, but I wouldn't take it. I was afraid it might make me unconscious, and I'd wake up and find myself without a foot. I had to be wake enough to argue the doctor out of the amputation when he finally arrived. I'm sure this must have been in-shock thinking, but it seemed real enough to me at the time, so I hung in until the doc got there and assured me he wasn't considering amputation. Only then could I safely take the pain medication and go to sleep for surgery.

It was a bad break, nonetheless. I spent several days with my leg up in the air for traction in that hospital, calling Freeman's ranch several times a day to talk with my children and see how they were. Collin hadn't come to visit me, so I'd assumed that was because he was having to take care of our two toddlers. However, whenever I called the ranch, I found that Collin had usually gone golfing or was off to somewhere else, sounded so stoned I could hardly understand him. My daughters seemed to be the only ones responsible for the two year old twins, and they didn't much like it. Neither did I.

The day I got out of traction was a turning point. I became so upset when I called and heard the babies' unhappy whining in the background, the girls fighting over whose turn it was to watch them, and learned Collin was at the golf course yet again that I hung up. I'd had enough and made my own decision. I needed to get us a place to stay nearby. Still crying and distraught, I started making phone calls. The hospital social worker came in and tried to calm me, but I told her to back off.

I managed to find a house to rent in Yucca Valley, fifty miles away – and home – then got hold of my sister, Bobette, who now lived Yucca Valley. She and her friend, Liz, drove down and collected me, cast, crutches, and wheel chair, took me to the Ranch where we picked up the kids, the VW Bus (to be driven by Liz) and our belongings and drove us to Yucca Valley. I had also called Salinas and told them about my ankle. The job there had involved traversing the barrio on foot, and I was no longer mobile. They'd hold the job open for me, they said, but only through the fall.

So there I was again, back in Yucca Valley, with no job, no Collin (good riddance) and with daughters who hated me for bringing them there, rather than letting them spend the rest of the summer at the ranch. Jimmy and Timmy were the only ones happy about being back in our hometown.

Things didn't stay that way for long, though. For one thing Collin was not so easy to get rid of. He showed up, suitcase in hand, a couple days later (it probably took him that long to realize we were gone), completely puzzled about why I'd made such a drastic move. He had things "under control," he said. "What the hell's the matter with you, anyway?"

So, after hours of talking that got me nowhere, I agreed he could join us. Trapped as I was in a wheelchair or occasionally on crutches, chasing down two-year-old twins wasn't going to be easy – and the teenagers in the house only did it for me with resentment. Besides, they needed some chasing down themselves at times. I knew I could use another semi-adult body in the house to help exert authority. And Collin was extremely good at exerting authority.

During a phone conversation about my accident with my friend Gary, he raised a question that stayed with me to ponder for several years. Even today, I'm not sure what the answer is. What he asked was, "I wonder why the Universe has to keep slapping you around so hard to get your attention." I'd never thought about the other accidents I'd had in that way and I remember being a bit miffed when he said it – but I couldn't seem to forget the question. My life had taken a 180 turn after the auto accident four years ago in '73 when I could no longer tolerate Daryl's presence – among other things; it took another turn with the birth of the twins, and now the broken ankle made it impossible to continue with my plans to continue with the Salinas job, at least at the moment. Were these things happening because I was exerting my will and not paying attention to signs the Universe was sending to counter them? Were they signs that I was heading down the wrong path – or were they simply random as I had always assumed? And how was I to tell the difference?

The following months went by in a blur. My pinned-together ankle took a long time to heal. Since without the Salinas job we had no income, I managed to get two night classes to teach at the local community college – somewhat local: I still had to drive twenty-five miles east to get there. And when my professors at the university learned that I was still in the area, they hired me for a half-time position teaching basic writing. That involved driving ninety miles west back to Riverside two days a week.

All this activity, of course, done on crutches and one leg in a cast up to my right knee, which is probably why the injury took longer than expected to heal. At least I was soon rid of the wheelchair. And the driving and teaching were easier than trying to tramp through the barrios on crutches. It seemed like a no-brainer to me.

Naturally, Collin fought against my taking the university position. All that driving would destroy our VW Bus, he said. I don't know how else he thought we would survive. He was reviving his sign-painting business, but – woo hoo – it only brought in two or three hundred a month. My half-time position paid as much as my graduate fellowship had, and I also knew that it would look good on my resume. As I mentioned earlier, full-time community college jobs in English had dried up in the state, and only by having previous and impressive teaching experience could anyone even be considered for the two or three openings a year. I knew the university position in Basic Writing, coupled with the adjunct community college teaching I was doing, was bound to enrich my resume. It was painful, but I made the call and sacrificed the job in Salinas since I couldn't have traversed the barrios until spring, and the organization couldn't wait that long.

Meanwhile, Collin and I were fighting daily, the teenagers were acting out all over the place – at school and home, and thirteen-year-old Jimmy and his new friends burgled a house for pot. I began writing poems about being eaten alive by my life and kids. By the time the spring semester was ending, we were facing a summer without my teaching income. I contemplated taking a waitress job again. After all, my cast was gone by now, and I only had a slight limp.

Chapter Nineteen
Reservations

I don't know where all this would have ended us up, if I hadn't gotten a call from Bobette, who was driving through the Navajo Reservation on vacation with Liz.

"I'm in Window Rock," she said. "God, it's gorgeous here. Red, red rock and green, green trees." I had a vague idea where the place was from drooling over maps of the area. Years ago, long before I went back to school, I'd wanted to take a long-cut through the reservation when Daryl and I went camping in Santa Fe. The wildness of the area had always intrigued me. Yet I knew the place was also a People's homeland, and I didn't feel comfortable zoo-viewing their lives. I had come to understand this as a child though my relationships with Indian George and his friends in the local desert tribes, which had given me great respect for indigenous cultures. So when we got home from that Santa Fe trip, I compensated by checking out all the books I could find on the Navajo and Hopi people from the library.

"I guess you're wondering why I called," Bobette said.

"I thought you called to lord your great trip over me," I said.

"Hah. Hah. That too. Anyway, Liz and I were reading the little paper here, *The Navajo Times*. There's an ad in it for a full-time English teacher at Navajo Community College in Tsaile."

"That would be quite a commute," I said.

"I think you ought to call the number and at least talk to them. I just have a feeling about this. Liz does too. The ad practically describes you. Got a pen?"

"I'm grading final papers. Got lots of pens here. Blue, green, black, red. Which do you prefer me to use? "

Bobette gave me the number, and after I graded a couple more papers, I broke down and made the call. Curiosity, hope, a sense of destiny, who knows? The English Chairperson answered, and we had an hour-and-a-half long conversation.

He was good enough to call me back on the college's dime after the first ten minutes. During the conversation I learned that *The Navajo Times* wasn't the only place they'd advertised and that they were getting calls from Harvard graduates. Nevertheless, by the end of the call, he had invited me to teach a five-week summer Upward Bound course (there was our summer money) as an interview for the fall-semester job. He said to bring my family. We could live in the dorms. Oh, boy. Collin was really going to love that!

It wasn't only Collin who was shocked about the idea, though it took a while before anyone realized I wasn't kidding.

"What is a Navajo reservation, anyway?" Jimmy asked. "How far is it?"

"No way, Mom," Kim said, looking down at the map of Arizona I'd picked up at the Circle K. "I'm not spending my summer in the middle of nowhere."

Timmy took one look at the map, then turned and went out the back door.

"I thought we were going camping," Linda said.

"I needed to find work *somewhere* this summer," I said.

"Can't you just leave us at the Ranch and you go?" Kim said. "You said we could spend *some* time there this summer."

"Not me. I'm not going back to the ranch," Jimmy said. "They hate me there."

"That's 'cause you took Silacyb's dope," Linda said. "You little thief."

"You all have to come. You need to see if you like the place, Kim. I might get a full-time position there for the fall."

"No way!" Kim and Linda blurted out in a harmony they never achieved anywhere else.

"That's easy. I can tell you right now. It sucks," Kim said. "There's nothing out there. God, not for hundreds of miles!"

"There's nothing at the ranch either, and you like it there," I said. Both girls rolled their eyes.

Collin said nothing while all this was going on. I'd half

expected him to try and squelch the whole thing in the beginning. We'd all been eyeing him, trying to read his reaction. Finally, he looked at me and said, "Well, I guess the money would get us through the rest of the summer. Not the full-time thing, though."

So the matter was settled, sort of, and without the fight with Collin I was prepared for. I checked out more books from the library, ones the Chair had recommended, and spent the next two weeks reading all I could find about Navajo culture, the no-eye-contact rules and soft handshakes and much else. Then we were off, sans Kim, who persuaded us to let her stay at the ranch, and Timmy, who at almost eighteen could safely stay home by himself. I hoped.

~

Those five-weeks at the Navajo college in *Tsaile,* Arizona were intellectually thrilling, and the teaching deeply satisfying. And it was foreign travel at its best. I'd taken several trips to Mexico and have since traveled to several European countries, but being on the reservation was much more foreign than any of those places. I'd had no idea that there was a whole other country right in the middle of ours – at least there was then, in 1978.

On a geographical level, I can't say the place actually *felt* foreign to me. In fact, I felt right at home. My geographical orientation there was almost as good as it was in the canyons of my childhood. I discovered I could make my way around through the piñon forest that surrounded the campus and arrive at the exact area on campus I was heading for. I felt as perfectly centered and in touch with the land as I had in Pipes Canyon, which assured me that I was right where I was supposed to be.

But the land around the college was much more stunningly beautiful than the desert land I called home. As I said, the college sat in the middle of a piñon forest, and the piñons graduated into tall ponderosa pines just before they reached the dramatic Chuska Mountains directly behind the college. The green of all those pines around the college was accentuated by the deep red of the clay-like sandstone soil, something I found soft and fine to place my bare soles upon. Just to the east of the college sat the breathtaking *Lukachuki Mountains*, huge round mounds of red sandstone rock out of which manage to grow green, green trees and a variety of plants of various shades. Over the next few weeks I would watch in wonder as several of my students ran along the dirt shoulder back and forth from the college to home in *Lukachuki*, some in running shoes but others on nothing but bare, and I assumed thickly callused, soles like mine had once been.

The area, *Tsaile*, (meaning roughly the rock that it flows from) was dominated by a volcanic plug and marked the beginning of the world famous, and locally infamous, Canyon de Chelly, (the name a corruption of tseyi, between the rocks) a place tourists come to visit from around the world. It is also the place where Kit Carson burned and ravaged peach trees and other crops to uproot the Diné people and force them into captivity in what the Diné call their long walk. I had learned the history of the Navajo's tragic interaction with White culture from books; now I was eager to learn what I could from this culture that had shaped itself around living harmoniously with the land long before we Whites had arrived. Although I had grown up living with wild land, I was aware that not much in the surrounding culture was in harmony with such land, and, in fact, was more likely to be trying to control and reshape that land, rather than to harmonize with it.

Collin and Jimmy were not as thrilled with our adventure, however. Surprisingly, Linda found it "interesting." The nearest grocery store was eighty miles away – off the reservation in Gallup, New Mexico. At least Collin could buy beer there, too – the reservation itself was dry, except for a few bootleggers who sold Bud at three to five dollars a can. (That meant lots of drunks on the highway driving back from Gallup.) There was no TV in the dorms where we stayed, although I saw antennas on some of the mud hogans and on the faculty houses, which were built of brick but round like the hogans. Luckily, the college library housed a huge collection of movies that the kids could access, and the college dorms had many video games for them to play.

Before we left Yucca Valley I had bought books and tapes on the Navajo language, which is incredibly complex and nuanced in ways unfamiliar to English speakers. I read that there were reputed to be a hundred thousand conjugations for the verb *to go*, depending on what was going, what shape it was, if it were coming back, if it had ever gone before, and so on. I didn't see how anyone with an IQ under two hundred could learn to speak that language. Still, I kept trying to produce the subtle sounds of the unusual consonants and to remember also how subtle distinctions in accent could change an appropriate word into one that could be either insulting or absurdly out of context.

I had hoped that once I was actually at the college, Navajo speakers would help to correct my mispronunciations and to let me know when I was speaking incorrectly, the way Spanish speakers were usually willing to do. I had always found most Spanish speakers happy to see that someone was actually trying to speak their language. Not so the Navajo, who would look at me without an expression of any kind to tell me I had said something either understandable or idiotic. It was as if my being a *bilagana*, or white person, cancelled my right to use their language. This was, of course, highly intimidating.

It soon became apparent that the most important things about interacting with the culture had been left out of the books I'd read. And, of course, the books had not dealt at all with how to teach in such a unique culture. None of the strategies I employed at the university or the community college, such as facilitating discussions, working and critiquing in peer groups, Socratic questioning were at all effective. Most clashed with cultural practices and mores, so from the first hour (the classes went five hours a day Monday through Friday), I found myself modifying normally effective strategies and trying entirely new ones. Part of the reason for this difference was because, whereas students in our culture are taught to compete to be the best, in the Navajo culture it is rude to stand out from the rest – so no one wanted to try to answer and questions I asked out loud in class.

Also the range of what *can* be asked without transgressing cultural norms is much narrower than in ours, something that I had no clue about. For example, asking the class, or a particular student to compare a practice depicted in a western-based story to a practice in their own culture might well transgress on rules about what can be revealed to someone of another culture – or at a certain time of year and even to certain relatives – if such a thing is allowed to be talked about at all.

Yet another reason I learned not to expect any more than a blank stare when I asked a student or class a question is that in Navajo culture there is no obligation to answer a question asked, at least not until the questioned person is ready. During my first week of teaching, I remember asking a student what she thought a line of dialogue in a story really implied. After getting nothing but a blank stare from her, I let it go and decided to give the students a study question handout I had made for the story and to let them work on it. Needless to say, blank-stare responses can be quite intimidating.

It was three days later that the student I'd asked the question of came up to me and thoroughly and thoughtfully answered the question I'd asked. The implications of this astounded me. It reminded me of a old Indian joke I'd heard but had never understood: Supposedly a cowboy passing through the desert comes across an old Indian man sitting beside a campfire. When the cowboy asks what the guy had for breakfast, all he gets is the now all-too-familiar blank stare. The punch line of the joke is that twenty years later the cowboy on his way back comes across the same guy beside the campfire, who looks up at the cowboy and says, "Ham and eggs." The connection between the joke and what had just happened with my student couldn't have been clearer if the student herself had said, 'ham and eggs."

Each day was full of experiences that brought such insights into the culture and each insight helped me to know better how to teach more effectively in that context. I loved the challenge to my creativity and intuitive sense, the challenge of teaching only "by the seat of my pants," and most especially loved the intense learning it brought to me. I had hoped for a different kind of learning about the culture, one gleaned from having students write about their personal experiences in the culture (something that normally works well with young college students but definitely not on the reservation), yet the kinds of learning I received on this new "reading between the lines" intuitive level was in its way much more satisfying.

By the end of the five-weeks, I felt entirely bonded with both the place and the culture and left for home with considerable regret. I was certain I would not be hired for the full-time job, even though, according to the English chair, I had done some spectacular teaching. But Jimmy had screwed it up for me by filching the same English chair's bag of pot while we were visiting him, and no amount of apology and cash payback would undo that little fiasco.

We started to settle back into Yucca Valley. I lined up classes to teach in the fall and renewed my half-time contract at the university. Then, surprise of surprises, the English chair called and said I had been hired full-time for the fall, the only glitch being that the administration said that they wouldn't provide housing for the new instructor they'd just approved. That was a pretty big glitch. There were no places for outsiders to live on the reservation, except in college housing. All the vast empty space "belonged" by tradition to families for grazing. And all the hogans were taken.

"That's okay," I said. "We can camp out next to the campus until they give in." An interesting full-time teaching job with health and retirement benefits was not something I was going to turn down for any reason. And I could clearly hear destiny calling. Or the place calling. And I'd never sought out places that were certified safe and secure. I knew I could handle rattlesnakes, both literal and metaphorical.

"I think the administration *will* give in, eventually," the chair said, "but there's no guarantee. I can't promise you anything. Honestly, I don't know what I'd do in your shoes." But, as usual, I had no shoes on; instead I'd been running my soles over the shag carpet, all the while imagining them meeting the soft clay of reservation sand as I ran along the road toward *Lukachuki*.

"I'll be there," I said."Come hell or high water." And I expected them both. I knew the experience would enrich the children, though I'd probably have to drag them out there kicking and screaming. And Collin? I hoped he was up for it, but, well, I'd go without him if I had to. This was one adventure I wasn't going to pass up.

"You got guts," the chair said. "And you're going to need them."

"I know," I said. "I'll need them on this end as well." Then I hung up the phone, took a deep breath, girded up, then walked out to break the news to my family that we were going back to live on the Navajo Reservation.

I knew a new life ahead when I saw one, and an adventure to boot. Of course, it could become a disaster for my family if housing did not come through. But something in me said it would come through. So, yes, on one level this was a conscious choice I was making. Even so, I was also following the dictates of some deep inner force that was far more powerful. Nothing short of another outside calamity was going to stop me – and, this time the forces outside, i.e., the Universe, as well as inside me appeared to be opening a door to this new life.

I wish I could round off my story nicely by having me head out to teach on the reservation of those bad-ass movie Indians, the Apache, whose tribe I pretended to be a member of so long ago. Instead, the truth will have to do. Real life doesn't smooth things off the way fiction does. Rough edges remain rough edges, and I really prefer it that way. What life does offer is far more rich and surprising than anything concocted by the human brain.

Acknowledgments

To begin with, let me acknowledge the fact that I no longer participate in the project to exterminate all rattlesnakes in my surroundings as was the case in the desert culture of my childhood when rattlers were overly plentiful around human habitations, drawn there by water, gardens, chickens, and rodents who were drawn there for these things as well. We all knew of people killed or crippled by rattlesnake bites; anti-venom wasn't in the picture; the nearest hospital was 70 miles away, much of it on dirt roads; snake kits were carried with us routinely.

I would also like to acknowledge that the material from my story comes from my experience as I remember it, which, as I know from reading research about memory, may subject to flaws.

I want to thank Carol Rawlings, Mary Sojourner, Bobette Perrone, and Nancy Nelson for their comments on the early draft of this work.

Thank you Dave Miller for the beautiful cover. Thank you Danny and Claudia Sall, John McMonagle, Stephanie Marler, Mike McMonagle – and especially Delilah Rose McMonagle for their part in the photo shoot.